THE DUTCH
HOW THEY LIVE AND WORK

HOW THEY LIVE AND WORK

Volumes in the series:

The Dutch

HOW THEY LIVE AND WORK

Ann Hoffmann

PRAEGER PUBLISHERS
New York . Washington

BOOKS THAT MATTER

First published in the United States of America in 1971
by Praeger Publishers, Inc.
111 Fourth Avenue, New York, N.Y. 10003
Second edition 1973

© 1971, 1973 in London, England, by Ann Hoffmann

Library of Congress Catalog Card Number : 72-144352

Printed in Great Britain

Contents

List of Illustrations

The following photographs are reproduced by courtesy of the *Government Information Service, The Hague*: pages 17 (bottom), 18 (right), 35 (top), 36 (top), 53 (top), 71, 90, 107, 108, 126 (bottom), 143 (left).

Acknowledgements

My grateful thanks are due to all those Dutch citizens—personal friends, government officials, press and public relations officers, as well as many private individuals—who have so patiently answered my questions and, in some cases, read and commented upon sections of this book in the making. While it is not possible to mention them all individually, I wish to thank especially Mevrouw E. Giesbers-van Kekem, in whose house the first chapter was written, and Mevrouw H. C. Rotgans-Rookmaker also for much generous hospitality, but chiefly for her sustained enthusiasm and assistance, which has included the reading of my manuscript during a severe illness. In this country I have benefited from the wise counsel of Mr Anton Zwemmer.

Monetary figures in this book have been calculated at the exchange rate of 8.70 guilders to the £ sterling and $ 2.40 to the £, except where they relate to the periods preceding the British devaluation of November 1967 and since the 'floating' of the guilder in May 1971. Current salaries, social security benefits, rents and prices are given in British decimal currency and at the approximate exchange rate of 8.40 guilders and $2.60 to the £ sterling.

General map of Holland

I

The Country and the People

'GOD created the world, but the Dutch made Holland.'

Every visitor to the Netherlands hears this popular saying sooner or later from the lips of his Dutch host or colleague. Invariably it is recited with great charm and an implicit element of exaggeration that cannot conceal patriotic pride in the achievements of a tough little nation which for over eight hundred years has battled incessantly against the North Sea for its very survival.

There is more truth in the old saying today than when it was first coined many years ago, reputedly by a Frenchman. For whereas the Dutch have been reclaiming land from the sea since the eleventh century—and had they not done so modern Holland would be barely half its present size—it is within living memory that the ambitious schemes have been initiated to drain the Zuyder Zee and to shorten and secure the coastline.

The kingdom includes not only the Netherlands in Europe, but also the former colonies of Surinam and the Netherlands Antilles. Eleven provinces comprise the Netherlands in Europe, or 'Holland' as the country is more commonly known—Groningen, Friesland, Drente, Overijssel, Gelderland, Utrecht, North and South Holland, Zeeland, North Brabant and Limburg. By the turn of the century there may be added a twelfth province, every square mile of which the Dutch people will proudly and without any exaggeration claim to have made with their own hands: the polderlands reclaimed from the Zuyder Zee. The

Dutch word *polder* means a tract of artificially drained land, usually protected by a dyke.

In this book the popular term 'Holland' will be used to describe the entire region of the Netherlands in Europe, stretching from Friesland and Groningen in the north to the provinces of Zeeland and Limburg in the south. Originally the word was *hol-land* (hollow, or soaked land) which in medieval days meant only the central part of the Low Countries, then one vast swamp. When the province of Holland emerged as the foremost of the United Provinces, the name gradually came to be used for the whole republic and later the kingdom. Officially still 'the Netherlands,' the country is known the world over simply as 'Holland.' Only those who live outside this province (now divided into North and South Holland) are sticklers for the correct use of the word : a Frieslander will talk of going to work 'in Holland'.

THE COUNTRY

Geographically, Holland lies at the centre of a circle of highly developed countries—the United Kingdom, Scandinavia, Germany, Luxembourg, France and Belgium. Bordered on the east by West Germany and on the south by Belgium (which once formed part of the same kingdom), the importance and prosperity of Holland as a trading centre have from the early Middle Ages to the present day derived, not from her size or natural resources, which are both small, but from her strategic position on deep navigable waters at the crossroads of western Europe.

Three great rivers flow through Dutch territory to the sea : the Rhine, the Meuse and the Scheldt. Slow moving, they deposit much silt in their estuaries, known as the Delta area. A northern distributary of the Rhine, the IJssel, drains into the former Zuyder Zee, now a freshwater lake and renamed the IJsselmeer. In the north-east, the Dutch-German border runs through the centre of the Ems estuary.

At present the country has a surface area of 15,750 square

miles, compared with 12,600 square miles in 1830. Large tracts have been reclaimed from the sea and more is being won each year. Two-fifths lie below sea level, in parts as much as 22ft below. Measuring at the longest point some 190 miles from north to south and at the widest 120 miles from east to west, Holland is less than one-third the size of England, or approximately one-seventh of Great Britain, and only just over half that of the American state of South Carolina. About 75 per cent of the land area, excluding wasteland and water, is under cultivation; one-fifth, approximately 2,850 square miles, is water, in the form of estuaries, lakes, rivers and canals.

For more than a thousand years the land area has fluctuated according to the dominance of sea or man. But for Dutch ingenuity in keeping the sea at bay, the coastline would probably now run down the centre of the country from Groningen in the north, through Utrecht to Breda in the south; the islands of Zeeland would not exist. Whenever the sea has encroached, man has drained the sodden land to reclaim his heritage, then built new dams and dykes to protect it; in the darkest moments of Dutch history the sea has taken its toll of land and human life, often destroying overnight the labour of decades. Although since the thirteenth century at least 1,500,000 acres of land have been reclaimed, in fact losses to the sea during the period 1200-1900, both along the coast and in the interior of the country, exceeded the gains by approximately 100,000 acres.

It should never happen again. Whereas in the past the face of Holland has been subject to change at the whim of the mighty ocean, from now on it seems that it will be changed only at the whim of the Dutch engineers. The dyke across the Zuyder Zee was closed in 1932, and reclamation work has been progressing ever since which, when complete, will have added 560,000 acres of fertile soil to Holland. The chain of dykes and dams of the Delta Plan, scheduled for completion in 1978, will constitute the strongest-ever defence against the water in the south-west. By the year 2000 the land will be more compact and more secure than it has ever been. Only then will geographers be able to draw a map of Holland with reasonable confidence that its outline will remain static for some time to come—at least until (and if) the more revolutionary schemes that are as yet still at the drawing-board stage come to fruition—but only for just so long as the Dutch maintain careful watch over their traditional enemy, the North Sea.

PHYSICAL CHARACTERISTICS

Holland belongs to the alluvial coastal region of the North Sea, part of the huge plain that once extended from Calais to Denmark. The Delta area was formed originally from layers of glacial deposits brought by the three great European rivers, while along the western and northern coasts the constant pounding of the North Sea waves on the sandy ocean bottom built up, over thousands of years, a substantial dune belt which now stretches the entire length of the Dutch coastline, from the Wadden Islands in the north to Zeeland in the south. Originally these dunes lay much farther west, but constant breaches made by the sea caused the separation of the islands from the Frisian mainland and hollowed out deep inlets in the southern region.

The dune belt and the rising wooded ground to the east and south of the country (only 1,000ft at their highest point) are alone above sea level. Between these two areas lie the low clay and fen lands, the polderlands that have been wrenched from the waters over the years and which, but for the elaborate system of artificial dykes and dams (once 2,000 miles in total, but already reduced to 1,250 miles) would be flooded at every high tide. Mountains there may not be, nor the vast rolling countryside of parts of England or the United States, yet in spite of the flat landscape there is a surprising variety of scene.

Texel, Vlieland, Terschelling and the chain of smaller islands off the Frisian coast known as the Wadden Islands, are wind-swept and stark, a haven for migrating birds. The miles of white sandy beaches running south from Den Helder to the Hook of Holland are backed by the dunes, which have a curious, wild beauty all their own. Most of this stretch of the coast is a pro-

ected area. Immediately behind the dunes lies a belt of wood-
and, which is fast becoming urbanised. The soil here is a mixture
of sand and peat—ideal bulg-growing country. The bulb fields
lie between Haarlem and Leyden, while south of The Hague
is the 'Westland' horticultural area where most of the hothouse
flowers and vegetables for which Holland is famous are culti-
vated. Further south, the industrial Delta area is dominated by
the Rotterdam-Europoort harbour complex, and beyond are the
picturesque islands of Zeeland, now linked together by bridge and
dyke and rapidly developing into productive, modern communities.

Behind the coastal area and a very narrow strip of old (as
opposed to reclaimed) land between Rotterdam and Amsterdam
lies 'Holland,' the low-lying central region. This flat polder
country, 50 per cent of the whole, fulfils every foreigner's image
of a typical Dutch landscape, where, cheek by jowl with housing
estates and factories, black and white cattle graze peaceably on
the rich grasslands, while fast-moving traffic speeds along nearby
roads, or more stately yachts and workaday barges ply up and
down the waterways above their heads. Here and in Friesland
and Groningen the country is so flat that it is possible to see for
considerable distances, and because there are so many lakes and
canals one is rarely out of sight of water.

To the south and east, the country becomes undulating but
somewhat less fertile. Pastureland gives way to shrub and heather,
to the orchards of the Betuwe district of Gelderland and the
woods of the Hoge Veluwe. There are superb stretches of
forest around Arnhem, near the German frontier. Brabant and
Limburg are a pleasant combination of meadowland and
woods.

The low-lying land was not always so much below sea level.
The early inhabitants of central Holland are held to blame for
what the Dutch call the 'rape of the earth.' In the east, when
they needed fuel, these people burned their woods; in the west,
having no woods, they dug up the soil, or peat. This was not as
disastrous as it might have been, for happily beneath the peat the
ancient clay soil proved to be exceptionally fertile.

This fertile layer of soil, which also occurs at the bottom of the lakes that have been drained, constitutes one of the country's few natural resources. Salt is another, a valuable residue deposited millions of years ago in the north and east, though in the west today the encroaching sea has created grave problems in regard to the desalination of drinking water and agricultural land.

Until a few years ago coal was the most important raw material, mined chiefly in the Limburg region. It has now lost out, partly to oil, which is present in small quantities in several districts, principally in the south and east and around The Hague, but more especially to the huge reserves of natural gas discovered recently in the northern province of Groningen.

THE STRUGGLE AGAINST THE SEA

Everyone knows the legend of the little Dutch boy who saved his country by sticking his thumb in a hole in the dyke. No one really believes this tale, but it points a moral. Never have the inhabitants of Holland been able to relax their vigilance over the sea.

The tribes which settled in the low coastal lands between

The Royal Dutch/Shell refinery at Pernis, near Rotterdam. The inauguration of a new crude distilling unit here in October 1968 made this the largest oil refinery in the world.

Dyke at Enkhuizen, on the former Zuyder Zee, typical of those all along the Dutch coast.

about 6000 and 4000 BC did little to combat the encroaching waters. They seem to have been content to live on higher ground along the dune belt, while the sea ate away the surrounding land under their very eyes. The Frisians who arrived in the fifth and sixth centuries before Christ were the first to construct defences. Settling in the marine clay belt of the north, they set to with hands and spades to make massive earth mounds or 'terps' on which they built houses and farms. There were once about 1,500 such terps, many linked together for greater security, some as high as 30ft above sea level. These first dykes, some of which still exist, were inhabited until about the year AD 1000, by which time the whole of Friesland had been encircled by a more sophisticated bracelet of dykes constructed under the guidance of the Romans.

Meanwhile in the south another centre of civilisation had developed on the peaty inter-coastal plain. In this marshy and hitherto uninhabitable district, some of the natural harbours were silting up, and the early settlers not only learned to construct primitive defences against the sea, but also devised a method of draining the land. One of the first polders was made there in about 1270.

None of these early precautions proved sufficient to withstand

---

Rotterdam : the rush hour begins : homeward-bound cyclists on one of the many cycle paths; café life on the Stadhuisplein, part of the Lijnbaan pedestrian-only shopping centre.

the sea, which was advancing steadily and closing round the land like two gigantic claws, one in the north, the other in the south-west. The fresh-water lake named by the Roman invaders the *Flevo lacus* or *Almere*, in the south of Friesland, was slowly penetrated by sea-water and its outlet widened so that by the year 1300 it had become the huge bay which for centuries has been the most distinctive and widely known physical feature of Holland, the Zuyder Zee.

The second claw of the sea swept in overnight on 18 November 1421, during a fierce gale. A vast expanse of fertile land was inundated, whole villages were wiped off the map and 10 per cent of the total population drowned. The horror of this disaster, which reduced Zeeland to a group of islands, has gone down in history as the night of the St Elizabeth flood. Part of the afflicted region, the Biesbos, which has become famous for its flora and fauna, has remained under water. The only flooded part of Holland not to have been reclaimed, in modern times this has proved to be an indispensable reservoir at critical periods when the waters of the Rhine and Meuse have risen above safety level. Under the Delta Plan, the Biesbos will become fresh water and ultimately will be reclaimed.

At the time of the St Elizabeth flood, the sea surged inland as far as Dordrecht, leaving a narrow strip only 36 miles wide between Rotterdam and Amsterdam. This small region, so very nearly submerged, became the centre of the low lands, taking its name of 'Holland' from the surrounding marshland and lakes left behind by the receding tides. Its existence was for many years precarious; until quite recently there was always a danger that some freak storm might breach one of the weaker dykes or that an exceptionally heavy rainfall would result in flooding. In spite of elaborate modern defences, Dutch engineers must always take into account that their land is sinking at the rate of a twenty-fifth of an inch per year and the average level of the sea is rising, so that even nowadays the danger is not altogether past. The dykes can never be strong enough.

'Impoldering,' or the conversion of submerged land into fertile polders through endykement and drainage, has been carried out

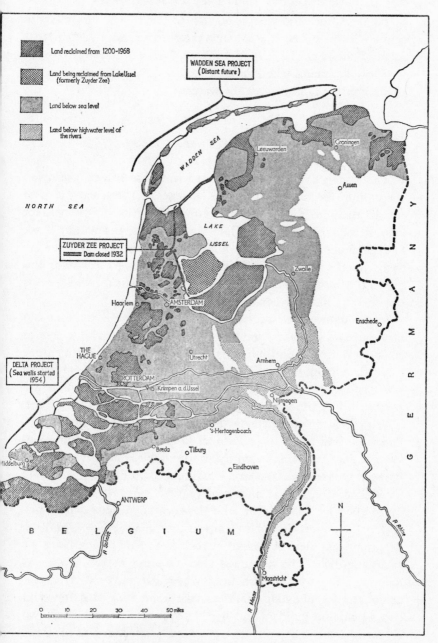

Land reclamation and land levels

in Holland since the year 1200. Up to the end of the sixteenth century it was purely a combative measure against the encroach-ment of the sea. The invention of the windmill made it possible to drain the inland lakes, an undertaking quite separate from the defence of the land against the waters.

LAND RECLAMATION

The Dutch have learned the hard way that behind the dykes there must be a second line of defence. Experience has also taught them that the lowland behind the dunes must be kept free of surplus rain water. The idea of using the windmill for land drainage was conceived in about 1350, and in the following three hundred years windmills were increasingly used for this purpose alongside the more primitive scoop wheels, which were operated by hand or horse.

In the sixteenth century there began the systematic drying out of various inland lakes, and the windmill was pressed into service extensively from 1600 onwards. By the mid-nineteenth century more than 9,000 windmills were working in Holland, although not all for land drainage purposes. Today some 900 mills are preserved in reasonable condition and 300 are still operational.

With finance provided by the wealthy merchants of Amster-dam who had made large fortunes in the Dutch East India and West India Companies, ring dykes were built round several lakes in north Holland and the land was drained within a comparatively short time. One of the most ambitious schemes was that drawn up in 1631 by an engineer with the curiously appropriate name of Jan Leeghwater (which means 'empty of water') to drain the Schermer lake near Alkmaar. It took five years to construct the encircling dyke. The reclaimed land, totalling 11,720 acres, was made into fourteen polders. Leeghwater also proposed the drain-age of the 14-mile-long Haarlem lake, estimating that it would cost $3\frac{1}{2}$ million guilders and would require 160 windmills. Two centuries later his plan was executed with the aid of three mechanical pumps.

The invention of the steam engine marked a great step forward; 45,000 acres were reclaimed from the Haarlemermeer between the years 1849 and 1852. Land reclamation was not, however, the primary object of this particular exercise; the lake had become (to use a Dutch expression) a *'water wolf,'* eating away its banks and spreading over the surrounding region, so that the slightest gale or heavy rainstorm constituted a serious threat to the neighbouring towns of Amsterdam and Leyden. It is on the bed of the former Haarlem lake, the scene of a number of bitter naval battles between the Dutch and the Spaniards in the sixteenth century, that Schiphol airport now stands, 13ft below sea level. The name 'Schip Hol' or 'Scheepsholl' probably once meant a hole, or hell, for ships. Parts of this region lie still deeper; this is the disadvantage of reclaiming land from the lake bottom.

The Zuyder Zee

As early as the seventeenth century a scheme was seriously considered for the reclamation of the Zuyder Zee, then a turbulent stretch of water covering a million acres. Thus three centuries before work was actually started the Dutch were looking towards that goal.

Plans were drawn up by Dr C. Lely, the most famous of all Dutch hydraulic engineers, towards the end of the nineteenth century. Its execution was held up by the outbreak of World War I, but in January 1927 work was started on the *Afsluitdijk*, or great barrier dam, which was to link North Holland and Friesland and shorten the coastline by nearly 200 miles. Simultaneously work began on the Wieringermeerpolder (50,000 acres), the first of the five great polders to be reclaimed from the bed of the former Zuyder Zee. It was completed in 1930, and the dyke was closed in May 1932. In April 1945 this polder was re-flooded by the Germans when Allied troops attempted to reach the dyke, but was pumped dry again by the Dutch six months later. The North-east polder (119,000 acres), begun in 1937, was completed under considerable difficulties during the war. East Flevoland (133,000 acres) was drained between 1950 and 1957. The most fertile of all the polders, it is estimated to have cost the government about £460 ($1,300) per acre, not including roads or other amenities. Of the remaining two polders, South Flevoland (107,000 acres) became dry in May 1968 and Markerwaard (150,000 acres) is still under construction.

The town of Lelystad on the western edge of the East Flevoland polder is destined to become the capital of Holland's twelfth province. On 1 January 1969 there were already 12,900 people living on the new polders. When reclamation is complete in about 1980, the surface area of the country will have been increased by 7 per cent, the arable land by 10 per cent. Some 300,000 acres of the Zuyder Zee will not be reclaimed, but will be used partly to provide recreational facilities and partly as a reservoir.

When it is realised that the soggy bottom of the former Zuyder Zee is unable, in an undrained or even partially drained state, to bear the weight of one man, the vast size of the scheme becomes apparent. Draining the polders is a magnificent achievement, but it is only half the story; the land then subsides, and, as a small amount of water tends to rise to the surface continually thereafter, a huge drainage system has to be operated round the clock in order to keep the land dry.

The Lauwerszee

In the north, work is progressing on reclamation of a stretch of water lying between Friesland and Groningen. Part of this lake, the Lauwerszee, is also intended for recreational use; the reclaimed land is to provide additional building land as well as possibly extensive military training grounds.

The Delta Plan

As soon as the Zuyder Zee scheme was under way, engineers turned their attention to the most vulnerable region of the southwest, where the 625 miles of sea dykes were both costly to maintain and by no means impregnable. Plans for the damming of the broader inlets were actually being studied when disaster struck on the night of 31 January 1953. A freak spring tide, whipped up by a fierce gale, breached the dykes and inundated large areas on a scale unprecedented since the 1421 flood. Some 400,000 acres of land were submerged, 1,800 people lost their lives and 72,000 had to be evacuated from their homes. The whole of central Holland, including the densely populated towns of Rotterdam, The Hague, Leyden and Delft, was at one time seriously endangered. But for the trojan work of those who toiled to close the breaches in the defences along the Hollandse IJssel— and succeeded only at the eleventh hour—the catastrophe would have been far worse. (The Hollandse IJssel is a tributary of the New Meuse, which it leaves just east of Rotterdam, flowing north to Gouda—not to be confused with the river IJssel.)

Three weeks after the disaster a Delta Commission was established; it recommended the immediate construction of floodgates and a lock in the Hollandse IJssel. Work began within the year and was finished in 1958. In June 1958 parliament approved the Delta Plan, a project which it is now estimated will cost about £345 million ($828,000,000). Basically the plan consists of the damming off of five deep estuaries, leaving open only the New Waterway and the Western Scheldt, which give direct access to the ports of Rotterdam and Antwerp respectively; here the dykes will be strengthened to provide maximum protection. Behind the sea dams there will be a line of three secondary dams. Three of the principal dams are already completed: the Brielse Maas, the Veerse Gat and the Haringvliet, which is the main outlet for the waters of the Rhine and Meuse. The Brouwerhavense Gat is due for completion in 1972. The final closure of the Eastern Scheldt, on which work has been progressing since 1966, is scheduled for 1978.

All three secondary dams are now finished; the Zandkreek in 1960, the Grevelingen in 1966, and the Volkerak, which has been designed with huge sluices to control the distribution of water, in 1970. Great flood defences have been constructed at Capelle-on-the-IJssel, while on the lower Rhine three adjustable barrier dams with locks will permit the surplus fresh water borne down the river when the mountain snows upstream melt in the spring to be diverted to the IJsselmeer. In the south there is to be another fresh-water reservoir, the Zeeuwsemeer, which will be fed mainly through the Volkerak sluices. In time the salination of inland waters will be brought completely under control. The bridge over the Eastern Scheldt, linking the islands of Schouwen Duivenland and North Beveland, was opened in 1968, and motorists may now drive over bridge and dyke from Rotterdam to Flushing and back without taking a ferry, cutting their journey by over an hour.

The future

As the long-drawn-out struggle against the North Sea continues, the Dutch are at last getting the upper hand. After the Zuyder Zee and the Delta Plan there is to come a third—the Wadden Plan—which aims to link the islands off the coast of Friesland with one another and with the mainland. Already it has aroused much controversy, in particular fierce opposition on the part of bird-watchers and others who intend to fight hard to preserve the islands in their natural state. Nevertheless, if approved by parliament, this gigantic project may well be realised during the first half of the next century. The estimate is that it will take 46 years to complete.

CLIMATE

Holland enjoys a marine climate, with moderate winters and cool summers. There are normally around 1,300 hours of sunshine a year, but on over 200 days out of the 365 the sky is overcast or there is some rain. Except on the coast, where the air is bracing, the atmosphere is often heavy, due to the low altitude.

The average day temperature ranges from 35°F (2°C) in winter to 64°F (18°C) in summer. Rainfall is usually between 25 and 35 inches a year, and it is not uncommon for as much as half this amount to occur during the spring and summer months. The prevailing winds are westerly and south-westerly, but in late spring cold northerly winds often sweep across the country. Mists and fog are frequent, especially in the autumn and winter months.

Occasionally, as in 1969, there is a long, hot summer. One of the predominant features of the Dutch climate is the exceptionally strong light on sunny days. Because much of the country is flat there is a huge expanse of sky, often with the most beautiful massed cloud effects, and the warm golden light at the end of a summer afternoon is very special. It is no wonder that Holland has produced so many great landscape painters.

The northern provinces tend to be colder than those of the central and southern region, the northern and western coastal districts wetter and more windy than the south and east. The winters are raw rather than intensely cold, although every few years there is an arctic spell when the lakes and canals freeze and the whole population seems to take to the ice on skates, transforming the scene into a Brueghel painting.

There are three predominant features of Dutch weather : the high winds that blow almost constantly in the western region; the all too frequent grey mist and driving rain; and its extraordinary changeability. Even in winter there may be snow or hail and ten minutes later blue sky and sunshine. A misty or wet morning often turns into a lovely afternoon, and the visitor would be well advised to do as the Dutch do—dress suitably, and then ignore the wind or rain. Unlike the English, they have learned to live with their climate and rarely make it a major topic of conversation. Exceptionally, in the summer of 1969 some were heard to complain that it was *too* hot; usually the most they will say is that their bad weather always comes from England!

RACIAL DERIVATION

Basically a Germanic race, the Dutch have always been exposed to influences from neighbouring countries. Thus many Hollanders are of mixed ancestry, for the long periods when their country suffered foreign occupation and her traditional open door to those fleeing from religious or other persecution brought the inevitable consequence of intermarriage.

When the Romans occupied the Rhine delta in 21 BC, two wild tribes of Germanic origin inhabited the region : the Frisians, who had previously ousted the Celts, and the Batavians, who were held by Julius Caesar to be the toughest and most warlike of all the barbaric peoples. Exhausted by the uprisings of these Frisians and Batavians and by continual attack from the Franks and Saxons, the Roman legions withdrew in AD 402. In time the Franks absorbed the Batavians, and three separate centres of civilisation developed : Frisian, in the north-west; Frankish, in the south; Saxon, in the north and east. From these three peoples the Dutch are directly descended.

Those of true Frisian stock are tall and blond, a pure Germanic strain, who consider themselves a race apart. The Batavians, also a fair-skinned, blue-eyed people, are well-built and muscular, with rather heavy features, characteristics to be seen everywhere in Holland today. By contrast, in the northern province of Groningen and in the east, Saxon blood has produced a race of smaller stature, with dark hair and brown eyes. In the south, and more especially in Zeeland, which was longer under foreign domination than the rest of the country, the Latin influence becomes apparent, both of Frankish and Spanish origin. This last is noticeable not so much in the colour of the hair, which may be light or dark, but in the somewhat finer features and gentler manners of the people.

Quite a number of Dutch people are proud to have Scots blood in their veins, being descended from the soldiers of various Scots regiments stationed in Holland during the sixteenth and seventeenth centuries, who fought for Dutch freedom and remained in the country. Many more are of Indonesian, Chinese or negroid stock.

CHIEF HISTORICAL LANDMARKS

The documented history of the Low Lands begins with the

Roman conquest in the year 12 BC, but prehistoric man probably lived in the eastern region near the present German border as much as 200,000 years ago. Later settlers, inhabiting the region some time before 2000 BC, utilised giant boulders left behind by the receding glaciers of the Ice Age as family tombs. Some of their megalithic graves still exist in the province of Drente.

Long after the Romans had withdrawn, Charlemagne (AD 742-814) subjugated the Frisians and Saxons. Under his Frankish rule Christianity spread rapidly. On the division of Charlemagne's kingdom among his grandsons, the Low Lands passed first into the kingdom of Lotharingia and subsequently into that of the Eastern Franks under the Saxon dynasty.

The next two hundred years saw the emergence of a number of semi-independent states whose lords owed allegiance to the German emperor. Friesland never acknowledged an independent hereditary ruler, but elsewhere in the Low Lands the old feudal link between vassal and king, and the power of the bishops, grew weaker. By the early thirteenth century the Counts of Holland had become the most important rulers of the region.

In 1384, the independent provinces were united under the Dukes of Burgundy. Under Philip the Good and his successor Charles the Bold they enjoyed a period of economic stability now known, largely through the work of the great Flemish painters, as the first 'Golden Age.'

Through the marriage of Charles's daughter Mary to Maximilian of Austria in 1477 the Burgundian Netherlands became part of the Holy Roman Empire. Maximilian's grandson, Charles V, later King of Spain and Emperor of Germany, added Friesland, the bishopric of Utrecht and the provinces of Groningen and Drente to his dominions. By 1543 he could claim that he ruled over 'seventeen Netherlands'—the extent of modern Holland, Belgium and Luxembourg. They provided the Hapsburgs with a handsome revenue.

Meanwhile, the writings of Desiderius Erasmus, the great scholar and humanist who was born in Rotterdam in 1466, were making a considerable impact all over Europe. When the full force of the reformation reached the Netherlands in the early sixteenth century, the doctrines of Martin Luther at first appealed strongly to the Dutch people, who were already critical of the Catholic Church and smarting under the Hapsburg yoke. Inevitably the cause of Reformation became tied up with the desire for liberation from the Spaniards. Hatred of their oppressors mounted under the brutalities of the Inquisition, which condemned to death thousands of patriotic, fervent Dutchmen convicted of heresy. Feeling rose to the point where Lutheranism and its rule of civil obedience was no longer acceptable; this led to the flowering of the Anabaptist movement and overwhelming support for the teaching of John Calvin.

A German-born prince, William of Orange, son of the Count of Nassau-Dillenburg, who had inherited large estates in the Netherlands as well as his principality in southern France, now emerged to lead the struggle against the Spaniards. Brought up as a Lutheran, but forced to become a Roman Catholic and to participate in the Hapsburg court at Brussels as a condition of being allowed possession of his Dutch estates, the Prince soon earned himself the popular nickname of 'William the Silent' through his ability to keep his mouth discreetly shut.

In 1555, Charles V abdicated in favour of his son, Philip II. An even more fanatical policy of persecution implemented by Margaret, Duchess of Parma, whom Philip appointed to act as regent, drove hysterical Dutch Protestant mobs to desecrate the Catholic churches. When the Duke of Alva was sent to restore order, Prince William, who by this time had openly professed Protestantism, led his army into the Eighty Years War. This struggle, which lasted from 1568 to 1648, was both anti-Catholic and anti-Spanish. The southernmost provinces supported Spain, but in 1579 the seven provinces of the central and northern Netherlands combined to form the Union of Utrecht. Five years later, William, who had been proclaimed the first *Stadhouder*, or governor, was assassinated at Delft by an emissary of Philip II. England attempted to come to the aid of the Dutch Protestants by sending a force under the command of the Earl of Leicester, but the mission was a political and military failure, although the subsequent defeat of the Spanish Armada by the English helped to relieve the pressure on Holland.

In 1588 the Republic of the United Netherlands came into existence, with William's son, Prince Maurice, as Stadhouder and the States-General as the governing body representing the seven provinces.

A twelve-year truce with Spain in 1609 heralded the start of the second 'Golden Age.' Denied access to Portuguese ports by Philip II, Dutch vessels now sailed direct to Java to obtain the spices previously shipped via Lisbon, the East India Company having been granted a charter for this purpose in 1602. The West India Company followed and in 1624 was instrumental in the foundation of a Dutch settlement on the American seaboard, Nieuw Amsterdam (now New York City). Colonies were founded in the East and West Indies, Ceylon and Brazil, and Holland became the shipping centre of Europe. Parallel with the new prosperity there was a flourishing of spiritual and cultural life. This was the age of the great painters, Rembrandt, Ruysdael, Vermeer, Jan Steen and Frans Hals, the poet Vondel, the composer Jan Sweelinck. The Portuguese philosopher Spinoza was one of many refugees who sought sanctuary in Holland. A group of English Puritans settled at Leyden, but fearing that the expiry of the truce would bring renewed fighting with Spain, they sailed from Delfshaven aboard the *Speedwell* in search of the New World. Subsequently transferring to the *Mayflower*, they reached the coast of New England in December 1620.

War with Spain was renewed in 1621. The capture of the entire Mexican silver fleet by the intrepid Piet Hein in 1625 provided the Dutch with much-needed finance for their campaign. The Peace of Westphalia, signed in 1648, formally recognised the independence of the United Provinces. A period of confusion followed, aggravated by much rivalry on the domestic front between monarchists and republicans. The great Princes of Orange, William I, Maurice, Frederick Henry and William II were all dead, and the government was temporarily in the hands of a grand pensionary (first minister of state), Johan De Witt.

The Dutch and English came to blows over supremacy at sea between 1652-4 and 1664-7. In the first of these wars the Dutch naval commanders Tromp and De Ruyter were forced to yield, but in 1667 De Ruyter's audacious raid on the river Medway, the only time that foreign guns have been heard in London, brought the conflict to an end. Under the Peace of Breda (1667), New Netherland in America (now New York State and New Jersey) was ceded to England; Surinam and Run (one of the Banda Islands) to Holland.

In May 1667 Louis XIV of France invaded the Spanish Netherlands and forced Holland, England and Sweden to band themselves together in the Triple Alliance. England changed sides in 1670, by concluding the secret Treaty of Dover with France, and twenty-one year old William III of Orange was appointed to command the Dutch army and navy in preparation for a grand onslaught. When De Witt and his brother were murdered in The Hague by an Orangist mob, William was appointed Stadhouder and accorded the full rights of his ancestors. He ultimately defeated the French and patched up the quarrel with England by marrying Mary, daughter of the Duke of York, later James II. In 1689, when James went into exile in France, William was crowned King of England.

The War of the Spanish Succession crippled Holland financially, and the emergence of rival powers in commerce and shipping marked the end of the country's 'Golden Age.' William died in 1702, leaving no heirs. Since John William Friso, a direct descendant of William the Silent and Stadhouder of Friesland and Groningen, was a minor and the other five provinces were not prepared to appoint him, control of their affairs was again temporarily vested in a grand pensionary. The House of Orange made a brief comeback in the mid-eighteenth century when Friso's posthumous son, Prince William of Orange-Nassau, who had married Anne, daughter of George II of England, was proclaimed William IV, Stadhouder of the Republic. His incompetence and that of his son, William V, whose Anglophile policy in particular fostered much resentment, led to the growth of a new democratic movement whose members styled themselves

Distribution of population in the Netherlands, 1971 (based on a map originally prepared by OECD in 1967). Some 4½ million people, about one-third of the total population, live within the area outlined in black, called the *Randstad Holland*.

'Patriots,' many of whom were sympathetic towards an alliance with France.

French revolutionaries invaded Holland in January 1795 and a few months later set up the Batavian Republic, which lasted only until 1806, when Napoleon Bonaparte appointed his brother Louis as King of Holland. In 1810 the vassal state was incorporated into the French Empire.

News of Napoleon's defeat at Leipzig in October 1813 inspired the Dutch to revolt. The son of William V was recalled from exile and proclaimed William I, Sovereign Prince of the Netherlands. The new kingdom included all the United Provinces and the Catholic provinces of the south. After a further struggle, the latter gained their independence and formed the kingdom of Belgium in 1839, together with part of the duchy of Luxembourg acquired by William in 1815—the rest of the duchy being administered by the Netherlands until 1867, when its sovereignty was vested in the house of Nassau.

The evolution of parliamentary democracy developed during much of the nineteenth century, the power of the sovereign shrinking as political parties came to the fore. In the period before World War I, prosperity returned to Holland through commerce and the development of her remaining colonial empire.

The enclosing dam across the former Zuyder Zee, 20 miles long and about 300ft wide at the waterline, varies between 22½ and 25ft above average water level. Originally designed for road and railway, the latter was never built and the dam is to be converted to take four lanes of traffic.

The Zeelandbrug over the Eastern Scheldt, with a span of 5,500yd, is the longest bridge in Europe.

Neutral in World War I, Holland was invaded and occupied by the Germans in May 1940. Queen Wilhelmina fled to London, where she remained in exile until the end of World War II; her daughter, Princess Juliana, went with her family to Canada. In 1948, three years after her return to liberated Holland and after almost exactly fifty years on the throne, Wilhelmina abdicated in favour of her daughter, the present Queen Juliana.

No longer a great colonial power, the present kingdom was established by a charter signed in December 1954 between the Netherlands and her former colonies of Surinam and the Netherlands Antilles. Indonesia became an independent republic in 1949.

POPULATION

It is ironic that with land at a premium Holland should have become the most densely populated country in the world. In 1900 she had a population of 5 million; today it totals 13,119,000, with an average of 1,020 persons per square mile. Since 1960 the annual increase has declined: in 1967, at 1 per cent it was lower than it had been since 1869 (except for 1945, an abnormal year, being the last of the war); in 1968 it rose again to 1.08 per cent.

Formality and informality: Her Majesty Queen Juliana opens Parliament; winter wedding party on the island of Marken, an ice dance.

The high birth rate and low death rate combine to make Holland's annual population increase the highest in Europe. A Dutch baby (there were 227,325 lives births in 1971) has an average life expectancy of 73.6 years, which is among the longest in the world. Not surprisingly, therefore, 10 per cent of the Dutch population are over 65, and more than 36 per cent under 19.

The trend is towards a higher percentage of males, although at present there are 1,003 women to every 1,000 men. Out of every thousand marriages, about 3.3 end in divorce and 0.3 in legal separation (called a divorce 'from table and bed').

About one-third of the population live in *Randstad Holland*, the low-lying polderland of the west. Embracing the three main centres of commerce, industry and government, Amsterdam, Rotterdam and The Hague, the *Randstad* sweeps in a near-circle to take in Hilversum, Haarlem, Leyden, Delft, Gouda and Utrecht, covering in all two-ninths of the whole country. Within this area the towns form huge concentrations of population. North Brabant and Limburg, being partially industrialised, are the next most highly populated provinces. Elsewhere the spread of population becomes thinner as one goes north, with an average of less than 400 inhabitants per square mile in Groningen and Friesland. Zeeland, until recently a series of separate islands, cannot boast much more, but her population is on the increase. The greatest potential, if not the only safety-valve, for the accommodation of the growing Dutch nation, lies on the new IJsselmeer polders.

After the last war, thousands of people returned from the Dutch East Indies. Many of them, Dutch citizens who had never seen Holland, later re-emigrated, mainly to the United States, Canada and Australia. Thousands have since returned to Indonesia. Between 1945 and 1969 455,000 Dutch nationals emigrated. Every year nowadays some 38,000 people leave their native country to settle overseas.

By 1980 it is forecast that there may be 14 million people living in Holland, possibly 18 million in the year 2000. Seven out of every ten Dutchmen are then expected to be living in towns of more than 20,000 inhabitants. How far the 'Pill,' now in widespread use, will affect this prediction remains to be seen. Final results of the 1971 census are not yet available.

LANGUAGE

Dutch is spoken throughout the country and a much older tongue, Frisian, only in Friesland. It is also spoken in northern Belgium and in the Netherlands Antilles; the Afrikaans language of South Africa is of Dutch origin, but is very different in grammar and pronunciation. The language is basically Germanic, with many words acquired from Latin and French but remarkably few from Spanish, considering how long the Spaniards dominated the country. In common with all European languages, modern Dutch has its full share of adopted English and French words and phrases.

Standard Dutch, known as ABN ('general cultural Dutch') is taught in the schools and used for all official purposes. Accents of course, differ regionally and among social groups. There are local dialects, some close to the standard and others almost incomprehensible outside the communities in which they are spoken. Along the German border and in Limburg, where there is a sing-song intonation, many German and French words are mixed with it. The language is peculiarly unattractive to English ears, a distinctive sound being the guttural, harsh 'sch.' Only the Scots can say this correctly. During World War I the name of Holland's principal seaside resort, Scheveningen, was used as a test word in order to discover whether a suspect was German or Dutch. (The Germans say a soft 'sch' and find it impossible to make the gargling sound in the Dutch way.)

Simplified, more phonetic spelling has been introduced since the war, but written Dutch still looks unpronounceable until it is realised that '*ij*' is treated as the letter 'y.' The Dutch have a passion for the diminutive '*je*,' which is added to many Christian names and nouns, as in *kopje koffie* (cup of coffee).

The Frisian language, which is of Celtic origin, is similar to early English and contains words like 'bread' and 'butter,' for which the Dutch equivalents are *brood* and *boter*. In Friesland it is spoken in the homes and taught as a second language at school; the rural signposts are bilingual. A Frisian may elect to speak his own language in a court of law and is entitled to the services of an interpreter.

NATIONAL CHARACTERISTICS

Many foreigners have written in an uncomplimentary vein on the Dutch character, ranging from the popular jingle, 'there's the Amsterdam Dutch, the Rotterdam Dutch and the other damn Dutch' to Lord Chesterfield's famous pronouncement, 'The trouble with the Dutch is that they offer too little and demand too much.' Of those who are wealthy but reluctant to pay, or too self-important, the Dutch themselves say that they always want to sit *voor een dubbeltje op de eerste rang* (in a front row seat for ten cents). It must be said that this has served them well in trade and commerce.

Perhaps what strikes the visitor most forcibly in Holland is that the people conduct themselves on a very even keel. Moderation and respectability are the keynotes in all aspects of Dutch life and among all classes of society. The true eccentric is comparatively rare; everyone (the new student generation excepted, but that is an international rather than national phenomenon) conforms to the same standards. Law and order are respected, flamboyance is frowned upon, temperament kept well under control. Thus the Dutch have come to be termed dull and unimaginative, especially by their more volatile Latin friends who find them both incomprehensible and at times exasperating. Their less spectacular characteristics of reliability, loyalty and industry are too often overlooked; their persistent curiosity and obsession with detail misconstrued.

Heredity and circumstance have made the Dutch stubborn fighters—in defence of their land, their personal freedom, their religious beliefs. Although by nature not an aggressive race, when roused they can be formidable opponents, bringing tenacity and loyalty of the highest order to their cause. Many British and American airmen and soldiers of the last war owe their lives to the outstanding bravery of the men and women of the Dutch Resistance.

Life has forced them to become realists. They set great store by material possessions, and they have learned to keep something in reserve against bad times. Yet they are not pessimists. Whenever the dykes have given way, the Hollanders have always set to with much spirit to repair and renew—without making a great song about it. Cheerful rather than gay, the face they show to the outside world is one of tolerance and good humour. This can be misleading, for they are not nearly so placid as they seem.

Their unsophisticated, sometimes rather crude, sense of fun comes closer to Anglo-Saxon humour than that of any other nationality, but unlike the English they lack the ability to laugh at themselves and are often surprisingly touchy. Nevertheless, they love practical jokes. A classic example of their down-to-earth humour dates from the rule of Napoleon. Ordered by their French master to register every citizen by a surname, the Dutch promptly retaliated by devising a list of absurdities. To this day their descendants continue to sign themselves *Naaktgeboren* ('born naked'), *Vanhetzelfde* ('of the same'), *Dodeman* ('dead man'), *Grizel* ('horror'), *Hogenboezem* ('high bosom') and many more such family names.

The influence of Calvinism is widespread and colours the lives of Protestant and Catholic alike. The education they receive in school and church, the strict principles on which they are brought up within the family, all combine to quell spontaneity and to clamp down on any tendency to excess. Past masters of the art of thrift, with a horror of living above their income, the Dutch are savers rather than spenders. 'Economy linked with industriousness will build houses like castles,' runs a Dutch proverb. Yet it has always been considered bad form in Holland to display wealth. In the seventeenth century the rich Amsterdam merchants did not build themselves the ornate castles they could well afford, but hid their prosperity behind a respectable façade of bourgeois houses along the *Heerengracht* ('gentlemen's canal'). It is equally impossible today to judge a Dutchman's financial standing from his outward style of living.

The impression must not, however, be given that the Dutch are a tight-fisted, miserly lot. They are in fact mean only with themselves. In the great causes of humanity they are the most generous of peoples—they have known too much disaster on their own doorstep to be otherwise. In everyday life there is nowhere on earth a more loyal friend than a Dutch friend, a more hospitable host than a Dutch host.

In looks they cannot be called a handsome breed, for they are in the main solidly built with heavy features, the womenfolk comely rather than beautiful. But here it is dangerous to generalise, for as in all composite races there is much variety. The true Dutch face, however, has changed little through the centuries, and the shopping centres of Amsterdam and Haarlem are thronged with men and women identical to those who were once portrayed by Rembrandt and Frans Hals.

The young are mostly of the open air, athletic type, with that kind of fresh complexion that unfortunately fades in middle age. The sobriety of dress of the older generation may be blamed on the climate or Calvinism or both. To be fair, can anyone look their best in beret or headscarf, with collar turned up against the wind?

The climate, and in particular the heaviness of the air, has often been made a scapegoat for the innate apathy of the Dutch people. It is true that they are not often stirred by great ideals or ambitions, but seem rather to be content with a middle-class existence. Sentimental rather than passionate, they bask in the glow of the family circle and are tempted not at all by the glamour and excitement round the corner. Shrewd as they are in business (the Japanese used to say that 'where a Dutchman has passed, even the grass does not grow any more'), to some extent the 'rat race' of the twentieth century seems to have passed Holland by.

Modern communications have practically levelled out the differences that once existed between the people of the various provinces. The westerners are, however, still considered to be the more rebellious, the easterners more peace-loving. The Frisians are said to be stubborn, the Rotterdammers the most hardworking, the people of Brabant easy-going. And while the Amsterdammer is loved for his good humour and the citizen of Utrecht gently teased for his old-fashioned, formal manners, those who live in The Hague (predominantly government officials with position rather than wealth) are regarded by their fellow countrymen as stiff and snobbish. Hence the well-known tales of the family which kept a wooden ham hanging in the kitchen for show and of the Hague professor who went regularly to the greengrocer to buy his potatoes, not with a shopping basket, but carrying an empty violin case!

In manners, the Dutch are a strange mixture. Courteous in speech and inveterate hand-shakers on greeting and parting, they push and jostle each other in shops and streets without a word of apology. Gregarious by instinct, their greatest pleasure is to visit or receive friends and relations. Unlike their famous prince, all are talkative (their one Latin characteristic), and the women especially have a propensity for lengthy telephone conversations.

Together with most western European countries, Holland has in recent years suffered a revolt of her youth versus the Establishment. The internationally famous *provo* movement of the early sixties has now been overtaken by the hippies, who have their centre in Amsterdam, but are far less in evidence there than their counterparts are in London. Serious street rioting took place, however, in August 1970, when the government banned them from sleeping in the Dam square. Styling themselves *Kabouters* ('dwarfs') and campaigning under the banner of *Oranje Vrij Staat* ('Orange Free State'), these young people then set up self-governing communities, or 'states within the State', in the major towns. In the 1970 municipal elections twelve of their 'ambassadors' (as they insist on calling their representatives) gained seats on the councils, five of them in Amsterdam. In spite of polling only 0.4 per cent of the vote in the April 1971 parliamentary elections, these 'sweet revolutionists' (they oppose authority, war and motor cars, but favour health foods and helping old people) still seek to obtain a voice in the running of the country's affairs.

Their main concern nowadays is with pollution and other environmental issues.

Less than forty years ago it was possible to draw a line across the centre of Holland and say that to the north the people were mostly Protestant, to the south Catholic. Today the southern provinces remain a Catholic stronghold, but the rest of the country has a fairly equal proportion of both creeds.

Preliminary figures for 1971 show that 39.5 per cent of the population are Roman Catholic, 30 per cent Protestant (23 per cent Dutch Reformed and 7 per cent belonging to Calvinist or other Protestant Churches). 22.5 per cent profess no religious belief, and 8 per cent belong to other denominations.

Happily, Catholic and Protestant no longer stand in bitter opposition, although the time has not long passed when Dutch Roman Catholics shopped exclusively at Catholic-owned shops, listened only to Catholic radio stations, visited only Catholic homes and voted only for the Catholic party (which they mostly still do)—and the Protestants likewise. Still mildly critical of each other, the two groups are nowadays moving closer together in political and other spheres.

The strict Calvinists tend to keep themselves apart, congregating in small communities, mainly in the northern provinces, where their rigid observance of the Lord's Day and their punishment of 'sinners' amounts almost to fanaticism. Only a few years ago a young woman suspected of adultery was dragged publicly through the streets of her native village. Members of certain sects have within living memory refused rescue from the flood waters, believing it to be the will of God that they should drown in order to atone for their earthly sins. Others have denied their children anti-polio vaccine (and farmers foot-and-mouth injections to their cattle), also on religious grounds.

More than 700,000 people living in Holland belong to sects or religious groups other than the Roman Catholic or Dutch Reformed Church. The bulk of the Jewish population of 14,500 (30 per cent of whom are refugees from other countries) is concentrated in Amsterdam. Here, before the last war, there were 86,000 Jews, of whom only 10,000 survived the Nazi extermination.

Officially, there is no religious discrimination. Years ago, however, following the war with Spain, Catholics were not admitted to government service, which is why so many shops were, and still are, Catholic-owned. Just over ten years ago, the appointment of a Catholic burgomaster in The Hague made history. Since then other Catholics have been appointed to administrative office in the Protestant north, and this is thought to have some bearing on the now steady drift of Catholics from the southern provinces.

A new liberalism is spreading through religious life in Holland. The Dutch Roman Catholics are the most progressive in Europe, not only in their recent defiance of the Vatican rule of celibacy for priests, but also in the modernisation of church services, which includes Mass said in Dutch and to the accompaniment of 'beat' music. Young people of different denominations are intermarrying more and more, and this too has influenced Dutch thinking. The ground is gradually being prepared for a change more far-reaching than anything that has occurred in the Church since the Reformation: the total acceptance of the ecumenical idea.

Nevertheless, as in many other countries, more and more people are moving away from the Church, both in political and private life.

2

How the Country is Run

WHEN the Kingdom of the Netherlands came into being in 1815, the monarchy was vested in the House of Orange-Nassau. It is hereditary in both the male and female line, but the latter only when there are no direct male heirs. In fact the male line died out in 1890 with William III, and until the Princess Wilhelmina, his ten-year-old daughter, attained her majority, Queen Emma, her mother, acted as Regent.

A Dutch sovereign is not crowned. The reigning monarch, Her Majesty Queen Juliana, was 'invested' on 6 September 1948, after 'the old Queen,' as her mother is affectionately remembered by the people, had with some difficulty, and only on the plea of failing health, persuaded the government to allow her to relinquish the throne. The end of Queen Wilhelmina's reign marked the passing of the old order.

In 1936 the Princess Juliana, as she then was, had married the German Prince Bernhard of Lippe Biesterfeld, now styled His Royal Highness the Prince of the Netherlands. Through the birth of three sons to their eldest daughter, Crown Princess Beatrix, who in March 1966 married Herr Claus von Amsberg, a German diplomat, the male line of succession now seems once more assured.

The Dutch royal family are among the most democratic in the world. At Soestdijk Palace, near Baarn, where they have made their home, a happy informality is maintained. The royal palace in Amsterdam is used by the Queen for only one or two days in the year, the Huis ten Bosch ('the house in the woods' near The Hague) for official functions such as the entertainment of visiting heads of state and the presentation of foreign ambassadors' credentials. A Dutch subject is not required to bow or curtsey to his Queen, and Court ceremonial has been reduced to the minimum. There is only one full-dress public State occasion during the year : the opening of parliament by the Queen on *Prinsjesdag*, the third Tuesday in September. While Prince Bernhard is most active in the spheres of trade and industry, science and the arts, the Queen takes a deep interest in the welfare and cultural life of her people. Her public appearances are often quite informal.

That is how the Dutch like their monarchy. Every citizen of Holland who pays his taxes considers that he has the right to see and talk to his sovereign, or certainly to write to her. On her birthday, 30 April, long queues of loyal subjects wait to file past the Queen on the terrace at Soestdijk to present their gifts and congratulations. This custom of taking flowers and other gifts to the Queen on her birthday originated in a spontaneous gesture made by the people of The Hague after the last war, when Queen Wilhelmina returned to her liberated country. One by one, plants and simple bunches of flowers were brought to the Noordeinde Palace in the town, where the Queen was then living, until the forecourt was one mass of blooms. That the tradition has continued ever since testifies to the esteem and affection in which the present Queen is held.

It is this deep respect of the Dutch people for their royal family that has helped them in recent years to weather such crises as that concerning the faith-healer consulted by Queen Juliana over the eyesight of her youngest daughter, and that of the controversial marriage of Princess Irene. The initially unfavourable reaction provoked by the marriage of Princess Beatrix to a German subject, mostly on the part of the older generation which had suffered so much during the war, soon faded. The integrity of Prince Claus is now established and he plays an increasingly popular role in his adopted country.

The constitution, which is binding on all organs of government and may only be amended by a Bill passed through both chambers of parliament, requiring the royal assent at each stage, lays down the basic freedoms of religion, of speech, of the press, and of association and assembly. It also strictly defines the powers of monarch and parliament, the judiciary, provincial and municipal administration. Amended on several occasions since it was originally drawn up in 1814—principally to change the composition of the two chambers of parliament and to extend the franchise—the present constitution dates from 1963.

THE STATE

The Crown is assisted by three advisory and administrative bodies—the *Raad van State* (Council of State), the *Staten-Generaal* (States-General, or Parliament) and the *Algemene Rekenkamer* (General Auditing Court)—which together comprise the High Colleges of State.

The supreme advisory body is the Council of State, presided over by the Queen. Its twenty members at present include the Crown Princess Beatrix, Prince Bernhard and Prince Claus. The Council cannot take administrative decisions on its own initiative; its sole function is to advise and to submit recommendations to the sovereign on all matters requiring a decision of the Crown.

Control over the State's finances is in the hands of the General Auditing Court, whose responsibility it is to scrutinise State revenue and report its findings to the sovereign each year. After submission to the sovereign, the report goes first to the Cabinet and then to the States-General and is subsequently published, thus giving the people the opportunity to judge for themselves the financial administration of their government.

The *Ministerraad* (council of ministers, or cabinet), which is the *de facto* executive, consists of the Prime Minister, the ministers and (since 1948) the secretaries of state, all of whom are appointed by the sovereign. Unlike in England, members of the Dutch cabinet do not sit in parliament. They have the right to speak there, but may not vote in either chamber.

The Queen and her ministers together constitute the government; under the constitution the Queen enjoys immunity but the ministers are responsible to parliament for the policy of the government. All royal decrees are signed by the sovereign and one or more ministers. Bills submitted by the responsible minister or ministers are discussed in the cabinet and laid before the Council of State by the sovereign before transmission to the lower chamber.

Members of the cabinet resign on the eve of the general elections, which are normally held every four years. The Queen, following consultation with her advisers (usually the vice-president of the Council of State and representatives of both chambers of the States-General), then requests a cabinet *formateur* to draw up a programme and to choose ministers who are prepared to serve. Only when this is accomplished does the Queen formally appoint the new cabinet. It is customary for the *formateur* to be appointed Prime Minister. Parliament is not required to approve either the composition of the cabinet or its programme.

THE STATES-GENERAL

The name of the Dutch parliament dates from feudal times, when representatives of the various estates were summoned by their lord to discuss revenue and other matters. During the Republic it was once described as a 'meeting of provincial ambassadors,' since representatives of the seven provinces, each of whom had one vote in the States-General, were instructed how to use their vote by the provincial estates. Although all provinces were held to be equal, by far the greatest influence was exercised by the province of Holland, and the parliament has traditionally met at The Hague, the seat of the former Counts of Holland. *'s-Gravenhage*, the Dutch word for The Hague, means literally 'the hedge of the Counts,' a reminder of the days in the early thirteenth century when the Counts of Holland maintained a hunting lodge near by and, in about 1248, built themselves a fine palace. When Count Floris V sold his rights to the throne of Scotland, he used the proceeds to add to his palace the Gothic

'Hall of Knights,' or *Ridderzaal*, where the State Opening of Parliament and other important government functions now take place.

The bicameral system has existed since 1815, the two chambers sitting separately in the *Binnenhof*, the inner court surrounding the Hall of Knights. Originally the lower chamber was elected by the provincial States, who were themselves elected by the three 'estates' of nobles, towns and clergy, while the upper chamber consisted of a body of gentry appointed for life by the sovereign, which in practice had little political significance but was useful to the sovereign as a blocking measure whenever the lower chamber went against his wishes. Direct suffrage based on a minimum payment in taxation was introduced in the revised constitution of 1848; since 1922 both the lower chamber and the provincial councils have been elected by universal suffrage of men and women based on a system of proportional representation. The upper chamber is elected by the provincial councils, but since both are now elected by the same electorate, virtually the same composition results.

One hundred and fifty members sit in the *Tweede Kamer*, or lower chamber, seventy-five in the *Eerste Kamer*, or upper chamber. The minimum age for a member of parliament is twenty-five, and no one may belong to both chambers. A president is appointed by the sovereign in each chamber, usually for one year. Members of the lower chamber serve for up to four years and may be re-elected. In the upper chamber, members are elected for six years; half of them automatically retire every three years, but become immediately re-eligible. The two presidents receive fixed allowances; members of the lower chamber draw an annual salary of £6,000 ($15,600) plus travelling expenses, while those of the upper chamber receive reimbursement of expenses in accordance with a fixed scale.

Bills are transmitted by the Queen to the lower chamber, where they are usually examined by a standing committee before being laid before the house. They then go to the upper chamber for approval and are afterwards submitted for the royal assent. Although the lower chamber alone has the right to amend, no

Bill may become law without the approval of the upper chamber. The right of the lower chamber to initiate legislation is seldom exercised. Parliamentary debates are open to the public and are occasionally broadcast or televised. Only rarely does the president of either chamber call for a secret sitting.

THE PROVINCIAL STATES

Under the 1814 Constitution the eleven provinces were regarded as independent administrative units dependent on the central government; the revision of 1848 gave them the management of their own provincial affairs. Today, under the revised Provinces Act of 1962, each province is governed by a representative assembly elected directly by the enfranchised inhabitants of the province. Elections are held every four years. The number of seats depends on the population of the province: in South Holland there are eighty-three, in Zeeland forty-three. They are divided among the participating political parties according to the proportional representation system.

Each provincial council has an executive committee composed of six members, charged with the day to day administration of the province, and also a Queen's Commissioner, appointed by the Crown, who acts as chairman of the provincial council and of the executive and is responsible for the maintenance of law and order. The commissioner and the executive together supervise the municipal administration and the district water boards within their province.

By reason of their autonomous position, the provincial states draw up individual budgets annually, which must be approved by the Crown.

THE MUNICIPALITIES

The unit of local government is the *gemeente* (municipality), of which there are over 900, incorporating every town and village in the country. The most ancient, Nijmegen, Maastricht and Utrecht, were founded by the Romans; the newest are those on the IJsselmeer polders.

Each municipality has a municipal council, an executive committee and a burgomaster. As in the case of the provincial councils, elections to the council are held every four years. The aldermen who sit on the executive are chosen by the council from among its members; they vary in number from two to six, according to the size of the municipality. The burgomaster is appointed by the Crown for six years; as well as being responsible for the maintenance of law and order, he controls the police, fire services and civil defence within his area.

All municipal authorities are subject to supervision by the provincial states and by the central government, but in practice the government rarely intervenes in municipal affairs.

Since the sphere of municipal activities is wider than that of the provinces, the budgets are considerably higher (an estimated annual total of £1,200 million ($3,120 million) compared with about £130 million ($338 million) for the provinces. Revenue is derived in both cases partially from the government, in the form of fixed contributions and direct grants for specific purposes, and partially from *opcenten*, or rates, which the provincial and

---

Workers in the tulip fields near Lisse.

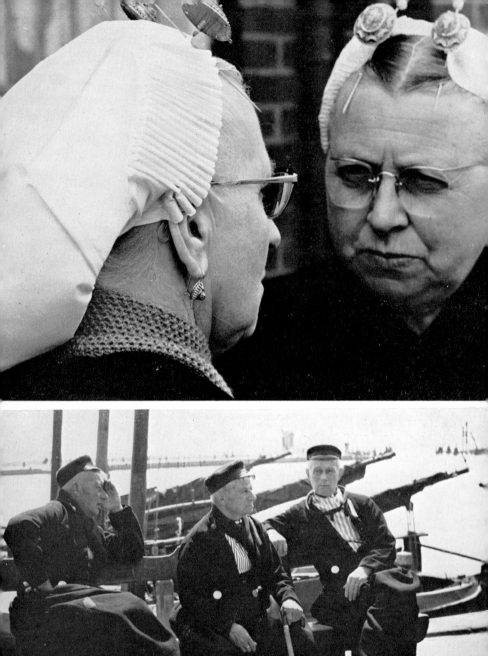

municipal authorities are entitled to levy from the taxpayer.

THE ELECTORAL SYSTEM

All Dutch subjects of twenty-one years of age and over who are resident in the relevant province or municipality on nomination day are entitled to vote in elections. A Bill lowering the voting age to eighteen should take effect in 1974. Elections for the lower chamber are not normally held in the same years as those for the provincial and municipal councils.

Compulsory attendance at the polling station was abolished recently, with the result that the parliamentary elections of April 1971 produced a turnout of 78.6 per cent of those entitled to vote, compared with the usual 95 per cent of previous elections.

The political parties submit candidate lists in each of the electoral districts or municipalities. For the purposes of general elections, the country is divided into eighteen districts; in the provincial elections each province is split into between two and ten districts, according to its size and population. Polling always takes place on the forty-third day after nomination day. Votes

-----

Wives of the Scheveningen fishermen still wear costume, but it is dying out among the younger generation.

Volendam fishermen, many of whom now find themselves without a job except dressing up for tourists.

D

are counted in public and the results sent to a central body, the Electoral Council, which works out the proportional vote and announces the outcome.

The electoral procedure for the upper chamber is almost identical, except that candidate lists are submitted by the members of the provincial councils and voting takes place at one of their sittings. The results are similarly worked out by the Electoral Council, and seats are allocated to the parties according to their proportion of the total vote.

THE POLITICAL PARTIES

There is an old saying, 'Place two Dutchmen in a room and they will found a debating society; gather three Dutchmen together in a room and they will found either a church or a political party.'

The Dutch political scene has long been characterised by its large number of parties based on religious and ideological principles. Since the war, however, there has been a marked change. There are fewer parties; the government is no longer predominantly right wing, and there has been a gradual diminishing of ideological differences which, coupled with the emergence of the welfare state and rapid technological development, brought about a definite waning of public interest in internal politics during the fifties and sixties.

The famous 'five pillars' on which Dutch society is said to rest—Catholic, Protestant, Socialist, Liberal and Communist —still stand, to a greater or (as in the case of the communists) lesser degree. New trends are the *rapprochement* of the two main religious parties and the marked decline in support for them. This has resulted largely from the vast upheaval of long-established values and the emergence of a new politically aware generation demanding more progressive party programmes and changes in the old social order.

As no one party commands a majority, every government is essentially a coalition. The principal parties are:

The Labour Party (PvdA), which, under its elderly but popular leader, Dr W. Drees, played a prominent part in post-war Dutch politics. One of PvdA's fundamental aims is to break down the existing religious divisions in politics. Between 1956 and 1967 the Socialist vote dwindled considerably, but in the 1971 elections PvdA gained 24.6 per cent of the total vote and became once more the strongest party in the lower chamber.

The Catholic People's Party (KVP) has formed part of the government continually since 1945, pursuing, on the whole, a moderately progressive policy. Until a few years ago, few Catholics voted for any other, but now that the right has been established to choose one's own party irrespective of religious affiliation, KVP's share of the vote dropped from 26.5 per cent in 1967 to 21.9 per cent in 1971. The party then held the second highest number of seats in the chamber.

The Liberals, or People's Party for Freedom and Democracy (VVD) was formed after the last war from the former Liberal party and a few dissatisfied ex-Labour members. Its economic and social policy is opposed to that of PvdA and rather more right wing than those of the religious parties. A stable, unified party which favours gradual change, VVD claims the support of 10.3 per cent of Dutch voters.

The two main Protestant parties are the Anti-Revolutionary Party (ARP), which believes that the country should be governed on strict Calvinist principles and regards the Bible as the one guide in political life, and the Christian-Historical Union (CHU), which is slightly less rigid than the ARP, with a membership drawn mainly from the Dutch Reformed Church. Both parties rely on all classes of the population for support; in recent years they have adopted a more progressive line and now favour collaboration between the three main religious parties.

Prominent among the minor parties is Democracy 1966 (D'66), founded six years ago by a group of intellectuals, dissatisfied with the established parties, with the aim of achieving a drastic reform (their own word is 'explosion') in the present parliamentary system. D'66 stood for the first time in the 1967 elections, when it gained seven seats in the lower chamber, unprecedented for a new party. Support continued to grow, and in 1971 D'66 held eleven seats.

The great surprise of the 1971 elections was the success of a new right-wing Labour party, DS-70, founded and led by Dr Willem Drees, junior, son of the former Labour Prime Minister. DS-70, which favours financial retrenchment and is critical of present economic policy, polled 336,000 votes and won 8 seats in the lower chamber; it was represented in the coalition cabinet.

Support for the Agrarian or *Boerenpartij* (BP), founded in 1959 by a group of right-wing farmers (*boeren*) in protest against government control of farming, has faded. They won only one seat in the 1971 election.

Among others are the Communist Party (CPN), which has never enjoyed much popularity in Holland, except immediately after the war; the Pacificist Socialist Party (PSP); the Radical Political Party (PPR); and two Protestant parties, the State Reform Party (SGP) and the Reformed Political Union (GPV), the latter being composed of right-wing Calvinists who just scraped two seats in the lower house. Relatively few of the minority parties that have come and gone in Dutch politics in recent years have been even moderately successful and are too numerous to detail here. Not that their record deters those who feel moved to break away from the existing parties and to establish other splinter groups : of the 28 parties contesting the 1971 elections, no fewer than 16 were new parties. Among these were the *Kabouters*, who, polling only 22,177 votes, failed to gain a seat in parliament.

In the 1971 elections the four former coalition parties (KVP, VVD, ARP and CHU) lost their overall majority, and only following protracted inter-party negotiations was a five-party coalition sworn in under a new Prime Minister, Mr Barend Biesheuvel, leader of the ARP. The new cabinet, politically right of centre, consisted of six members of the KVP, three each of ARP and VVD, and two each of CHU and DS-70. Only three of the ministers had held office in previous governments. The PvdA, while not represented in the cabinet, continued to exert considerable influence in parliament.

As this book goes to press it is announced that new elections, not normally due until 1975, are to be held in November 1972.

Raging inflation and other sources of political discontent had rendered the Biesheuvel government's position difficult from the outset. After a near-defeat over the issue of raising university fees, crisis point was reached in July 1972 when DS-70 withdrew from the cabinet in disagreement over proposed cuts in government expenditure. The government, no longer commanding a majority support in parliament, resigned. It took Mr Biesheuvel four weeks to form a new minority coalition consisting of the three confessional parties and the Liberals—the latter party accepting office only on the promise of early elections. This temporary government, with the support of only 74 out of 150 members of the lower chamber, had the task of getting the new budget proposals through parliament before the country went to the polls.

If the necessary legislation can be enacted in time to allow the 18-year-olds to vote at the forthcoming elections, the outcome will certainly be interesting, and possibly unexpected.

THE CIVIL SERVICE

Except in legislative matters, the government and the civil service function to a large extent independently of parliament. The Prime Minister's role is primarily one of co-ordination. Principal policy decisions are taken by the Council of Ministers, over which he presides. The States-General can, however, call ministers to account for all actions falling within their individual responsibility.

There are at present fourteen ministries; General Affairs, headed by the Prime Minister and comprising the secretariat of the Council of Ministers and the Government Information Service; the office of the Vice-President of the Council of Ministers, which has special responsibility for matters concerning Surinam and the Netherlands Antilles; Foreign Affairs; Justice; Education and Sciences; Finance; Home Affairs; Defence; Housing and Physical Planning; Transport, Water Control and Public Works, which also supervises the postal, telephone and telegraph services (PTT); Economic Affairs; Agriculture and Fisheries; Social Affairs and Public Health; Cultural Affairs, Recreation and Social Welfare.

In 1970 there were 218,597 persons in government service. This figure includes 62,029 in the PTT and 24,642 workers engaged on a contract basis, as well as 122,631 in regular salaried positions in the various departments. Although the average Dutch civil servant used to call himself 'overworked and underpaid,' salaries have risen steeply within the last twenty years and now compare not too badly, at least in the higher grades, with industry and the professions.

WATER CONTROL

Holland has a unique system of water control regulated by law. The District Water Control Boards represent one of the oldest forms of statutory body in the country. They are established and supervised by the relevant provincial state, except where sea defences and the major rivers are concerned, in which case they are appointed by the Crown. Overall responsibility lies with the Ministry of Transport, Water Control and Public Works, but the ultimate authority in all matters of water control is the Crown.

Each board is governed by an executive committee, which is elected by the land or property owners of the district, and is responsible for all matters relating to water control within its particular area and for the construction and upkeep of certain roads, bridges, viaducts and other public works. Revenue is obtained by the taxation of landowners and through subsidies from the provincial authority or central government.

CURRENCY

The monetary unit is the guilder, or florin, which in May 1971 was floated on the foreign exchange market in an attempt to curb inflation. The intention is ultimately to return to the par value of 3.62 guilders to the United States dollar.

In 1936 the Netherlands was the last to abandon the gold standard. The guilder has since been devalued once, along with the pound sterling (1949), and revalued once (1961). It now ranks with the US dollar, the *Deutsche Mark* and the Swiss franc among the hardest currencies of the world. When Britain devalued in 1967, Holland was not forced to follow suit; in the autumn of 1969 she withstood the revaluation of the German mark.

The guilder is divided into 100 cents. Paper money is issued in notes of 1000, 100, 25, 10, 5 and 2.50 guilders. Silver and nickel coins in circulation are the 2.50 guilders (still known as the *rijksdaalder* from the pre-1937 days when it was almost the equivalent of one US dollar), the 1 guilder, the *kwartje* (25 cents) and the *dubbeltje* (10 cents). The last two coins have been minted only in nickel for some years. At the lower end of the scale there are the two copper pieces, the 5 cents or *stuiver* and the one cent. In May 1970, to mark the twenty-fifth anniversary of the liberation, a restricted number of ten-guilder silver coins were issued.

Because the silver content of the coinage now exceeds its face value, since July 1968 it has been illegal for any individual to export more than twenty-five guilders in metal coin.

The Dutch bank rate has been progressively lowered in the last two years: from 6 to 5½ per cent in April 1971, and to 5 per cent in September the same year; to 4½ per cent in January, and to 4 per cent in March 1972. Comparative rates are (1972): United Kingdom, 5 per cent; United States, 4¾ per cent.

TAXATION AND GOVERNMENT EXPENDITURE

With the government expenditure for 1972 estimated at over £300 ($780) per head of the population, it is not surprising that the Dutch are among the most heavily taxed nations of the world.

The taxation system is both complicated and severe, and one has every sympathy with the man who recently walked into an Amsterdam tax office, took off all his clothes and told the outraged officials, 'You might as well have these too!'

Income tax is payable on a resident's entire income, according to a sliding scale, after certain deductible expenses have been allowed. A new system of inflation-linked adjustments in the tax scale became effective in January 1970. Tax deducted at source from all wages and salaries is offset against a person's final assessment for the year, which includes a real estate tax based on the sale value of property, a personal property and rental tax, a tax on share and bond dividends and a wealth tax. The earnings of a married woman are tax-free up to £100 ($260) a year only; above this, and up to a maximum deduction of £500 ($1,300) the tax is 20 per cent and any earnings over the maximum are added to her husband's taxable income. While her position has improved, there is still little incentive to a wife to work. The real estate tax is currently 4.86 per cent on buildings, 6 per cent on land; the personal property and rental tax 3.4 per cent of the annual rental value plus 1.5 per cent of the value of the furnishings (with certain deductions allowed for depreciation etc). On top of these government taxes, the surtax percentages (rates) levied by the municipal and provincial authorities can add as much as 200 per cent to the taxpayer's bill.

Wealth tax is levied at the rate of 0.6 per cent above £4,750 ($12,250) for an unmarried person, or above £7,500 ($19,500) for a married person, with additional allowances for each child, for invalids and those over sixty-five.

To give an example of the kind of tax a Dutchman pays, as at 1 January 1972: with a taxable annual income of £1,000 ($2,600), if unmarried, he would pay approximately £105 ($273) under the age of forty, £100 ($260) between forty and sixty-five; over the age of sixty-five, or if married without children he would pay £75 ($195), with one child, £50 ($130), with three children, £25 ($65), and with four or more children no tax at all. On a taxable income of £2,500 ($6,500), an unmarried man under forty would pay £625 ($1,625), a man with five children less than

half this amount. A man with ten children (not all that uncommon in Holland) would pay tax only on income exceeding
£2,200 ($5,720). Rates rise steeply in the higher income group:
an unmarried man between forty and sixty-five would part with
almost half an annual taxable income of £10,000 ($26,000).

The tax on directors' fees has now been abolished, but cor-
porations are subject to a net profits tax of 43 per cent up to
about £4,750 ($13,350), rising on a sliding scale thereafter.
Other taxes include death duty and a duty on gifts, a lottery tax,
motor vehicle tax (which depends on the type and weight of
vehicle), a tax on various legal fees, and customs duty on
certain imported goods (special arrangements exist between EEC
and Benelux member countries). Television licences are obtained
from the post office, dog licences from the municipal authorities.
Polder tax, paid by owners of property or land on the polders, is
levied by the district water boards.

The value added tax on goods and services which came into
force in 1969 as part of the system of tax harmonisation between
the EEC countries, has replaced the 'turnover' tax as the main
form of indirect taxation. On 1 January 1971 the supplementary
tax on cars was raised from 15 to 18 per cent and VAT in general
from 12 to 14 per cent, with no change in the 4 per cent on basic
foods. Prices have rocketed and the impact of this tax has been
felt by the whole of the population, as well as by foreign visitors
who can no longer count Holland as one of the more reasonable
countries of Europe.

Public expenditure has increased a hundredfold in the last sixty
years and now accounts for between 32 and 33 per cent of the
national income. Total tax revenue in 1970 amounted to 28,666
million guilders, compared with the intermediate figure of
33,100 million guilders for 1971. The 1972 estimate is 37,500
million guilders.

Among new measures introduced in 1971 and continued in
the budget estimates for 1972, to meet the worsening economic
situation, were substantial cuts in State spending and a *wiebeltax*
(special fluctuating tax) which will add roughly 4 per cent to the
average taxpayer's bill and to tax revenue for the year.

DEFENCE

In May 1940, not having fought a war for over a hundred years, Holland was mentally unprepared. Today, as a member of the North Atlantic Treaty Organisation, of which Dr Luns, the former Foreign Minister, is now Secretary-General, she spends 3.9 per cent of her gross national income on defence.

All young Dutchmen have to attend a medical examination at the age of eighteen and, unless exempted, are called up for national service within the next two years. As there are now too many young men of conscription age—about 120,000 per year as against the annual service intake of 55,000—thousands are granted exemption, usually where two brothers have already been called for national service, or on medical or other grounds. They remain liable for service in the event of war. About 85 per cent of those conscripted are drafted into the army, 5 per cent into the navy, and 10 per cent into the air force. The maximum time of national service is twenty-one months in the navy or air force; in the army, reserve officers, NCOs and specialists serve for eighteen months, the remainder for sixteen months. After national service they are 'on reserve' and may be called at short notice to attend periodic refresher courses.

The average peacetime strength of the Royal Netherlands Army is 95,000 men. Holland's present land force commitment to NATO consists of an army corps of two 'combat ready' divisions and several mobilisable units, of which a nucleus only is available in peacetime but one of which can be mobilised and made 'combat ready' within a few days. These Dutch NATO-assigned land forces form part of the Northern Army Group, which has its headquarters at Mönchen-Gladbach in Western Germany. Holland is desperately short of military training areas, and some of her M-day units are stationed and trained in Germany. In a few years' time, however, the army will take possession of land either in the Lauwerszee area or in east Groningen. Its equipment is modern, and a fleet of German Leopard tanks will shortly replace the British Centurions now in use.

As well as the NATO land force, Holland has a territorial defence system for the guarding of key installations against surprise attack. Also several army units serve in Surinam. There are three guards regiments which carry out normal peacetime duties in addition to their ceremonial duties on State occasions; the Rangers, or 'Green Berets,' who undergo a tough commando-type training; also the Royal Military Police, whose duty it is to guard the royal family and the frontiers and, if required, to control military traffic. Regular commissioned officers of the army and air force are trained at the Royal Military Academy at Breda.

Holland suffered heavy naval losses in the Pacific during the war, and since 1945 the Royal Netherlands Navy has been completely rebuilt. Its striking force consists of the cruisers *De Ruyter* and *De Zeven Provinciën*, the latter having been re-equipped with guided missiles. Twelve destroyers, six frigates armed with the latest submarine-tracking apparatus, six submarines and a number of patrol vessels, supply and training ships, patrol ships and anti-submarine aircraft carriers make up the full force of 130 vessels. The construction of two anti-submarine frigates is to start shortly.

In the event of hostilities, the Dutch Navy is bound to join other NATO members in protecting overseas supply routes to western Europe under the two NATO commands, the Supreme Allied Commander Atlantic (SACLANT) and the Channel Committee and Channel Command (CINCHAN). The main naval base is at Den Helder, where there are a naval dockyard and the Royal Marine Institute for the training of naval officers.

The Royal Netherlands Air Force used to be attached to the army. An independent service only since 1953, it now forms an integral part of the NATO air defences. The force consists mainly of jet fighter-bombers and interceptors divided into air defence and tactical air command, two squadrons for air defence equipped with F-104G Starfighters, four squadrons of F-104G Starfighter bombers and Northrop NF-5A fighter-bombers (which have replaced the F-84F Thunderstreaks), one reconnaissance squadron, a transport squadron and three squadrons of light aircraft suitable partly for air rescue purposes. There are also two four-squadron groups equipped with Nike missiles and three four-squadron groups equipped with Hawk missiles stationed in Germany.

The training command works in conjunction with the Belgian Air Force, and after an elementary course in Holland, flying personnel go to the air base of Brustem in Belgium to train on the Fouga Magister jet. Belgian and Dutch pilots then receive advanced training together on Northrop NF-5B two-seater planes at the Dutch air base of Twenthe. Formerly many Dutch pilots were trained in the United States and Canada.

Women may volunteer for service in the army, navy and air force, where they are known as MILVAs, MARVAs and LUVAs respectively.

THE LAW

The Dutch legal system differs from those of the United Kingdom and the United States. Trial by jury has never existed in the Netherlands: the administration of justice and the application of the rules of criminal law are in the hands of independent professional judges appointed by the Crown.

The country is divided into nineteen judicial districts, in each of which there is a court of first instance competent to hear both criminal and civil cases. Within these districts there are altogether sixty-two lower courts, which are also courts of first instance but have jurisdiction only in minor criminal cases such as traffic and fiscal offences or the infringement of municipal regulations, and in civil cases where claims do not exceed approximately £100 ($260). Appeals from the lower courts are heard in the district courts, and ultimately in the Supreme Court at The Hague; appeals against sentences passed by the district courts are heard in one of five High Courts (sitting in Amsterdam, The Hague, 's-Hertogenbosch, Leeuwarden and Arnhem) and, in the last resort, in the Supreme Court.

Criminal proceedings may be instituted only by the Department of Public Prosecutions. Under the supervision of the

Minister of Justice, this department works through the five attorney generals at the High Courts, who in turn control the public prosecutors and their deputies attached to the district courts (but in practice give them a rather free hand). A public prosecutor is not bound to bring an action; when he fails to do so, however, an aggrieved party in a criminal case may petition the competent court of appeal. In major criminal cases and in the civil courts three judges sit together; in minor criminal cases they sit singly. There are exceptions in certain civil cases, where evidence may be heard by one of the three judges. All judges, and the Attorney General, are appointed for life.

Where police investigation has failed to establish a *prima facie* case, evidence may be heard in camera before an examining magistrate prior to trial. Consequently, the fact that very few witnesses are usually called in open court makes Dutch trial procedure seem a little dull in comparison with that of Britain and the United States. Every person is entitled to legal representation in court, and where a defendant's income is below a certain level the State pays for free legal aid.

There are special tribunals to deal with administrative disputes. Civil law cases are frequently decided by abitration; military personnel are tried before courts martial and have their own appeal court.

CRIME AND PUNISHMENT

In Holland, as in so many other countries, crime is on the increase. The rate of detection, however, has fallen in the last ten years from just over 50 per cent to around 45-46 per cent. Murder and sexual crimes are comparatively rare, but major theft and burglary have mutiplied and here the detection rate is only 25 per cent. The recent wave of bank robberies and organised crime is thought to be master-minded by known professional criminals from Germany and other countries, who have taken advantage of relaxed frontier controls to infiltrate into Holland and have imbued the Dutch underworld with their aggressive ideas.

Drug traffic is centred in the cafés of Amsterdam. Public opinion on this problem is divided; in university circles there is open support for the free availability of marijuana and even LSD. The government recently announced an easing of the law on the use of certain 'soft' drugs.

Capital punishment was abolished in 1870. The courts are empowered to impose penalties other than prison sentences, and the Dutch penal code and other statutory instruments lay much emphasis on rehabilitation and the psychological needs of the offender. Special provisions relate to criminal psychopaths, young adults and juvenile delinquents. Penalties in general tend to be less severe than in the United Kingdom, and it is rare for the maximum sentence to be given. The State is responsible for the administration and maintenance of all penal institutions. Much of the rehabilitation, medical care and judicial child welfare work is, however, deliberately kept in private hands, although heavily subsidised by the government.

THE POLICE

There are two separate forces: the State police, under the authority of the Minister of Justice, which performs general police duties throughout the country in over 850 municipalities which do not have their own force, and the municipal police, controlled by the burgomaster of the municipality. Municipalities of more than 25,000 inhabitants maintain their own police force; those of 10-25,000 may have either a State or municipal force.

The combined strength of the municipal police is about 15,000; that of the State police about 7,000, which includes water and air police sections, a central specialised traffic force and a State detective force. A municipality bears the cost of its own police, sometimes with the aid of a grant from the Minister of the Interior. The State police are financed by the Ministry of Justice.

The State police do not intervene in a municipality where there is an independent force unless its support is requested by the municipal police. In an emergency the Royal Military Police may be called on to assist either force.

INTERNATIONAL LAW

In the tradition of Grotius, the 'father of international law' (Hugo de Groot, 1583-1645), Holland has become the world centre for the settlement of international disputes. The Permanent Court of Arbitration, established in 1899, and the International Court of Justice, which is the judicial organ of the United Nations, both have their seat at The Hague.

3

How They Live

HOUSING

BECAUSE the Dutch spend more time in their homes than most other Europeans, they also spend a greater proportion of their income on making their living quarters *gezellig* (the translation for which is 'cosy,' but in Dutch it means much more, really a way of life). A Dutch woman often seems to take more pleasure in some new item for her home than in a new dress.

The Hollander's greatest ambition is to have a house and garden; flat life has been forced on him mainly since the war. Failing a garden, and even if the home is just a couple of rented rooms, there is nearly always a balcony or a *serre* (veranda) at the back of the house to be made into a conservatory.

———

Typical gallery flats in Rotterdam Zuid.

'One-family' houses at Emmen, in the province of Drente.

Indoor plants and flowers are a feature of every living-room.

Children are much in evidence in a Dutch household. They normally live with their parents until they are twenty-one or until they go to university or to work in another town; many stay in the family home until they marry. Only since the war has it become generally acceptable for unmarried daughters who are earning their own living to leave the parental roof. Some universities have special student flat accommodation, but many live in rented rooms or share flats with fellow students. At the other end of the scale, few of the elderly live with their children, as is the custom in France. Preferring to be independent, they usually arrange several years in advance, in accordance with their means, to move to an old people's home, a service flat or *rusthuis* (private home especially for the elderly) when the time comes that they are no longer able to live alone.

Visitors often remark on the rows of identical brick terrace houses (the Dutch call them 'one-family' houses) all over the country and, in the *Randstad* and newly-developed areas, the apartment blocks all built to the same pattern—mostly with galleries along the front and distinguishable one from the other only by different coloured paintwork on the doors or façade. The reason is not a lack of imagination, but one of expediency; with

––––––––

The town hall of Bolsward, in Friesland, one of the Dutch Renaissance-style treasures, built in 1613-17.

A *hofje*, or almshouse, at Hoorn, one of over 200 in the country, most of which were founded in the early seventeenth century and still provide homes for the elderly in a picturesque, tranquil setting.

E

90,000 homes totally destroyed during the war, the use of standard component parts and a rationalised system of building were essential ingredients in the post-war reconstruction programme, in order to provide housing quickly and at low cost. That the two millionth dwelling to be built since 1945 was actually completed in 1971 gives some indication of the speed at which building has taken place, and it is hardly surprising that a certain uniformity predominates.

Multi-storey flats have appeared on the scene only comparatively recently, and as far as foundations permit they are getting higher. Not by American standards, though—for in Holland a fourteen-storey building is considered very high, most apartment blocks having about six storeys. There has just been completed an extension on to the 392ft high Euromast tower in Rotterdam, constructed in 1959-60 to afford the public a panoramic view over the city and docks, a view which was fast becoming obstructed by tall buildings. At present Holland has fewer flats in proportion to her population than any other country of western Europe.

Before the war, every family wanted a house, but most middle-class townspeople lived in *etage* or *portiek-woningen* (two-storey houses containing ground floor, first and second floor flats). Only the wealthy could afford to live in the blocks of flats then built, usually the luxury type with restaurants. After 1945, people had to find accommodation where they could, often cramped in rented rooms, sharing kitchens and washing facilities. It was at this period that many of the older town houses owned by the well-to-do before the war were converted into flats. The fifties and sixties produced a wave of middle price apartment-block building, and it became the 'in' thing to live in a flat. Recently there has been a pronounced turning away from flats and back to the 'one-family' house.

The average number of persons per household has dropped to 3.6, which is still high compared to other European countries, and most new houses and flats are being built with an average of 5 rooms including the kitchen. (In West Germany the norm is 4.3 rooms; in France, 3.5.) One- and two-roomed flats are now built only for elderly or single people. The typical Dutch worker's flat today probably has a floor area of around 615sq ft and consists of a living-room, two bedrooms, a kitchen, a shower and washing unit, and a lavatory. There is normally at least one balcony and basement storage space for bicycles and fuel.

The basic layout of the 'one-family' house has not changed since before the war. Inside the front door there is always a vestibule large enough to accommodate the bicycles belonging to the household. Coats are hung in the inner hall, which has a tiny cloakroom, often built in the space under the stairs, with room only for a lavatory and wash basin. The living-room runs from front to back of the house, nearly always with sliding doors to divide the front sitting section from the dining section, which sometimes has a hatch through to the kitchen. Upstairs there are two or more bedrooms and a bathroom. Kitchens and bathrooms are small by British and American standards; in many cases bathrooms and toilets do not have an outside window.

The cosiness of the Dutch interior is unsurpassed anywhere in the world, but to British tastes the living-rooms are often overcrowded. The older generation still clings to the traditional and rather heavy style, with solid antique furniture, fringed velvet curtains, ornamental gilt-framed pictures and an abundance of Persian rugs (often draped over tables or hung on the wall); the young favour the more functional Scandinavian type of interior decoration. Books, ornaments, lamps and indoor plants fill every available niche; bedrooms, in contrast, are sparsely furnished. Great importance is attached to lighting, and electric light is the one commodity with which the Dutch are lavish; most people leave their living-room curtains undrawn in the evening, a custom which dates from 1945, when the lights went on again after the wartime blackout. It has been suggested that as they all lead such highly respectable lives they have nothing to hide; be that as it may, the Dutch, with their inborn curiosity, like to know how their neighbours live. To the visitor, the lighted windows are welcoming and friendly in a strange town.

Windows are bigger, cleaner and more flower-filled here than anywhere in the world. It is rare indeed to come across one, at least on the front of the house, that does not have plants or flowers on the windowsill. Net curtains—if any—are usually draped or parted to let in the maximum sunlight. Window cleaning is a weekly ritual, along with the other scrubbing and polishing that give the Dutch housewife her unparalleled reputation for spotlessness in the home. It used to be said that a Dutchwoman spent more time and was more fastidious over her windows and her doorstep than she was over her person, but nowadays, when nearly all houses have hot and cold running water and at least eighty-five per cent have bathrooms or showers, this is certainly not true—and has not been found so in the author's own experience! The fact remains that the women of Holland do take an excessive pride in keeping their houses clean and tidy (*netjes* is their own excellent and much-used word for it), and since few of them have a career after marriage, it occupies their time.

Bedclothes used to be thrown half out of the window each morning to air—sometimes the mattress, pyjamas and nightdress as well. There is still the ritual of vigorously beating all carpets and upholstery in the garden or on the balcony, but this old custom too is dying out. Even today, however, nothing compares to the *grote schoonmaak* (spring cleaning), about which the Dutch housewife has an absolute mania. A couple of generations ago there were rigid rules about finishing it in the week before Easter (this is still practised in Friesland); nowadays it is planned to coincide with the end of central heating. For the two to three weeks while it is in process, home life is disrupted and it forms the sole topic of feminine conversation.

Holland is a country renowned for cleanliness, yet dogs foul the pavements almost unchecked and the public is no more litter-conscious than in London or New York. Of course the wonderfully clean air helps (fingernails and net curtains do not get nearly so grubby as they do elsewhere), and the work of the public cleansing authorities is ably supplemented by the wind and rain which blow the rubbish away and wash down the streets. For the rest, it is the neatness of the farms and gardens, the sparkling windows and the fresh paint on the doors and shutters (white on the new houses, dark green picked out with red on the traditional-style buildings) that really catch the eye and give the country its well-groomed appearance.

HOUSING STATISTICS AND REGULATIONS

In 1971, a record total of 136,595 houses and flats were built in Holland. The target for 1972 is 132,000 per year, and if this can be maintained it is expected that the housing shortage will be over within ten years, even allowing for the fact that the number of new households requiring accommodation is likely to increase to 72,000 a year in the 1970-80 period.

Under the Housing Act of 1965, a permit is required for every building project, and strict regulations are laid down concerning government subsidies and the improvement of poor housing conditions. Roughly 84 per cent of the total housing programme is subsidised : 45,000 dwellings a year are wholly financed by the State, built by housing associations and municipalities on a non-profit-making basis for rental to those in the lower income group; and 55,000 are privately built, usually by a bank or insurance company; the government pays an annual subsidy for them in order to keep rents to a reasonable level in accordance with the income of the occupants. Those wishing to build their own houses can usually obtain an 80-90 per cent loan at very low interest, the State guaranteeing the repayment of the loan to the lender. An additional 25,000 dwellings a year come into the 'free' sector, a more luxurious type of accommodation built to the individual's own specification and financed entirely by him, but which must conform to certain technical requirements.

The slums of Rotterdam were wiped out in the bombardment of May 1940, when virtually the whole city centre and the docks were destroyed. Some slums still exist in Amsterdam and other towns, but out of 375,000 of these sub-standard dwellings at least 250,000 are scheduled for improvement; the remainder will be demolished within the next few years. Many of these condemned houses are already empty.

Holland has no real homeless—only an estimated one hundred and fifty vagrants in the entire country.

Rents were frozen in December 1940. After the war, in order to maintain an equilibrium between old and new housing, all rents became subject to strict control. The less crowded regions are now gradually being freed from these measures. Pre-war rents come under the Rent Act of 1950 and have since been fixed annually at a percentage based on the 1940 level. They vary considerably according to the district and category of accommodation, but since 1950 they have increased by roughly 330 per cent. In the case of new houses and flats built with government subsidies, maximum rents are fixed by the Minister of Housing and Physical Planning; in all other cases landlord and tenant are free to come to a mutual agreement, and in the event of dispute may ask the advice of a rent tribunal as to the legal rent. The Act protects tenants from eviction except by court order. A 6 per cent annual rent increase became law in 1969.

One problem now facing the government is the large number of people who are living in accommodation below the level they could afford, it being felt that approximately one-sixth of a person's income might reasonably be spent on rent. No legislation has yet been enacted, but some means will be sought soon, either to get these tenants to move, and so free the cheaper housing for the less well-off, or to make them pay a rent tax.

Before the war, the majority of Dutch people lived in rented accommodation; today 33 per cent of the housing is owner-occupied. Rents are much lower in the country districts than in town. A pre-war 'one-family' house in the *Randstad* may be rented for £20-£40 ($52-$104) a month, depending on the area; a worker's two-bedroomed flat in, say, The Hague, for £12-£20 ($31-$52); a luxury flat in town might cost as much as £100 ($260) a month. The new 'one-family' houses may be purchased for a small down payment on a long-term mortgage (twenty to thirty years) of up to 90 per cent. Such houses cost anything from £8,000 to £20,000 ($20,800 to $52,000), those near the big towns being about double the price of houses in the country.

In the immediate post-war years the local authorities had

power to requisition dwellings, and the Housing Accommodation
Act 1947, which made it illegal for anyone to move house without a permit, was enacted in order that what little housing was
available should be allocated as efficiently as possible, without
discrimination against those of limited means. As the situation has
eased, restrictions have been gradually abolished. In the densely
populated west, however, it is still necessary to seek permission
from the *Huisvesting* (housing authority) before moving. This is
now largely a formality, and there is no longer any shortage of
flats in the higher price range, even in the larger towns.

One household in twenty-five owns a second house. The craze
for a *tweede woning*, which began in about 1959 with the conversion of cheap agricultural labourers' cottages in Drente and
Gelderland, and quickly spread to old farmhouses in Friesland
and Groningen, has led to a steady demand for new chalet-
bungalows, of which there are already 4,000 and will be 8,000
by 1975. Motor cruisers, luxury yachts and caravans account for
seventy-five per cent of the present total of 150,000 second homes,
which cost their owners anything from £500-£20,000 apiece
($1,300-$52,000), plus tax. By 1985 it is forecast that there will be
600,000 such homes, and by the year 2000 double that figure,
one for every four and a half families. Some 190,000 acres of
space will be needed, and for the sake of the landscape all such
houses will in future be built only in special bungalow parks.
Each chalet costs in the region of £3-£5,000 ($7,800-$13,000).
Very occasionally an old cottage in Friesland, suitable for conversion, may be found for around £500 ($1,300), a farmhouse for
£3,000 ($7,800). The 'prestige' value of owning a second house,
which is usually about one or two hours' drive from town, is
enormous.

HOUSING THE ELDERLY

Since the war Holland has taken special measures to house
her elderly people, most of whom are encouraged to live in
specially designed houses or flats in order that they may retain

their place in the community. Sometimes these dwellings are grouped together to form a centre where the old people may live independently but also enjoy community social facilities and be given hot meals and some domestic help. In the period up to 1 January 1970, 51,688 such dwellings were built. Most belong to municipalities or private bodies and are subsidised by the State. Old people whose capital is less than a certain amount may apply for financial assistance.

For those with independent means there are luxury service flats. They are expensive (a three-room flat might cost as much as £7,000 [$18,200]), and there is a monthly service charge to cover heating, hot meals and maintenance which may amount to £50-£80 ($130-$208) for a married couple. Other accommodation is available in residential homes, where old people may have one or two private rooms and take their own furniture. 593 homes of this type have been built since the war and 183 existing homes improved and extended. Some 4,000 people, mainly women alone, are housed in *hofjes*, or almshouses.

About 71.4 per cent of Holland's elderly folk live independently, 7.6 per cent in old people's homes or boarding houses, and 21 per cent with relatives.

HOUSEHOLD EQUIPMENT

Central heating is a feature of nearly all new housing, even that designed for the lower income occupant. Some older people retain the traditional stove in the living-room, but more and more are converting to oil or gas heating. Open fires, where they exist, are for show, to be lit only when entertaining guests, or as a supplement to normal heating.

All blocks of flats more than four storeys high have lifts. Many also have chutes for the disposal of kitchen waste and other rubbish. Virtually all housing nowadays has running water and indoor lavatories, and it is compulsory to build bathrooms or shower units in all new houses and flats.

The modern Dutch housewife is well equipped with electrical

appliances to ease her domestic chores. Seventy-five per cent of all households have a washing machine, 45 per cent a refrigerator. The most universal kitchen gadget is the coffee grinder—the Dutch are particular about their coffee, and over 99 per cent of all housewives grind their own. Forty per cent have the telephone, compared with 22 per cent in the United Kingdom and 71 per cent in the United States.

DOMESTIC HELP

Few families have servants living in. Some upper-class households employ a daily or general help, but most get by with a *werkster* (charwoman) on one or two half days a week, a window cleaner once a month and some regular help in the garden. Demand still exceeds supply, but the fact that rates of pay have increased recently has tempted some working men's wives back to work for a few hours a week, so that it has now become slightly less difficult to obtain help. A *werkster* is paid about 60p ($1.55) an hour in the town, less in the country.

SOCIAL SECURITY

All Dutch residents between the ages of fifteen and sixty-five are insured under the General Old Age Pensions Act (AOW), which came into force on 1 January 1957. A contribution of 10.3 per cent is deducted from salaries and wages up to £2,500 ($5,330) a year. No extra premium is payable on income above this maximum, and there are concessions for self-employed persons with low incomes. Where a person is not employed, the contribution is levied by the tax authorities.

Pension rates rise annually with the current wage level, and there is talk of bringing them up to the fixed minimum wage of an unskilled worker. The present rate is approximately £50 ($130) a month for a single person, £70 ($182) for a married couple, payable from the age of sixty-five.

Under the General Widows' and Orphans' Pensions Act of

1959 (AWW), widows without children receive benefit equivalent to that of the single old age pensioner, and those with children under eighteen to that of the married couple. If a widow is over forty at the time of her husband's death, or if she has unmarried children or is unable to work through disability, this pension will be paid until she qualifies for the old age pension; younger widows without children are entitled to benefit only for six months. Orphans are granted pensions according to their age, ranging from just over £16 ($44) a month under the age of ten to £30 ($78) up to twenty-seven, provided they are following some full-time education.

Family allowances are payable for the third and subsequent children, on a sliding scale (just over £20 [$52] a quarter for the third child up to £34 [$88] for the eighth and subsequent children). Everyone is entitled to this allowance, regardless of income. Self-employed people whose income is below a certain level (currently £1,050 [$2,730]) may claim an allowance for the first two children, which wage earners automatically receive.

Seventy per cent of the population participate in a *Ziekenfonds* (health insurance fund). This is compulsory for all employees whose earnings are less than £2,250 ($6,500). Employer and employee each contribute 4.1 per cent up to a maximum daily salary of £7.50 ($19.50), and the families of the insured person are fully covered. Those who are not employed but whose income falls below the same maximum may also participate, on payment of a fixed voluntary contribution, usually about £1 ($2.60) a week for a single person or £1.85 ($4.80) for a husband and wife. Children under the age of sixteen, students and disabled children are insured free. A system of voluntary contributions payable by the elderly, based on income, up to a maximum of approximately £1,500 ($3,900), ranges from about 65p to £2.25 ($1.70 to $5.85) a week; it is obligatory for health insurance funds to insure them. Contributions are deducted from benefits paid to widows and orphans, the unemployed and disabled who are thus compulsorily members of a *Ziekenfonds*.

Participation in a health insurance fund gives the right to free medical treatment. Half the cost of simple false teeth is covered; spectacle lenses are free, the patient contributing only a nominal sum for ordinary frames. In 1970 it was estimated that each *Ziekenfonds*-insured person cost the State about £23 ($60).

The new General Special Sickness Expenses Insurance Act (AWBZ), introduced in January 1968, provides for the free treatment of prolonged or special sickness for all persons living in the Netherlands, regardless of income. This entitles a person to free treatment in any recognised nursing home or institution for the physically or mentally handicapped, from the day of admission, or in a hospital, sanatorium or psychiatric institution from the 366th day after admission. Those who wish to be nursed in a better class establishment need now only pay the difference between what the State would cover (third class) and the cost of a private room. No contributions are paid by those in receipt of widows' or orphans' pensions, and the over-65s pay only a nominal sum per month after a year's hospitalisation. Everyone else must contribute 2 per cent of their annual income up to £2,250 ($6,500) a year. In the case of wage-earners this is paid by the employer.

The total cost of payments made under the social security scheme amounts to some 23,595 million guilders annually. Of this, 22.05 per cent is covered by employers' contributions and 18.85 per cent by those of employees.

Many Dutch people participate in private pension schemes, and nearly everyone who is not insured with a *Ziekenfonds* has a private medical insurance.

MEDICAL CARE

The average *huisarts* (general practitioner) has a list of 2,750 patients, private and *Ziekenfonds*. There is no real shortage of medical personnel; out of a total of 18,000 medical practitioners in the country, 4,500 are 'house doctors' (GPs), 6,000 specialists, 3,000 dentists, and the remainder are physicians working as medical officers, factory doctors or in some similar capacity.

For every *Ziekenfonds* patient up to 2,000 a doctor receives a *per capita* sum regardless of how often he is consulted. Insured persons choose their own doctor and are entitled to free medicines; they may not however choose their own specialist, but must abide by the choice of their doctor in this respect. There is no fixed tariff for private patients. £1.50 ($3.90) is normal for a consultation at the doctor's surgery, £1.75 to £2 ($4.55-$5.20) if the doctor visits the house. A first consultation with a specialist may cost around £5 ($13), subsequent visits £3 ($7.80). Dentists' fees vary from £3 ($7.80) for a simple treatment to £25 ($60) or more for, say, a gold crown. Surgeons' and anaesthetists' fees vary according to the class in which a patient is insured.

The cost of a hospital bed varies with the size and equipment of the institution (there are several categories of hospital) and the class of room chosen. Few hospitals nowadays have first-class rooms, which may cost as much as £16 ($41.60) a day; this includes medicines and drugs, but not operating or medical fees. A second-class private room costs around £14 ($36); a room for two patients, £12.50 ($32) per bed; for four patients, £10 ($26) per bed. In the third class, where *Ziekenfonds* patients are treated free of charge, the daily cost is around £8 to £9 ($20-$23). Modern hospitals have a maximum of five or six patients in the third-class wards, but some older hospitals still exist with as many as twenty beds in one ward.

Most of the 268 hospitals are run by private organisations, on a denominational basis. About a quarter of the country's total of 70,000 beds are in State (provincial or municipal) hospitals. The thirty-nine mental hospitals can accommodate about 28,000 patients. Nursing staff is not as short as it was a few years ago, for they are now well paid; 17,000 registered nurses and 18,000 student nurses are employed in the hospitals.

Home nursing and preventive medical care generally is in the hands of private bodies such as the Green, White-Yellow and Orange-Green Cross associations, which are subsidised by the government and local authorities. Over 2,500 baby clinics and

2,000 child welfare centres are staffed by these associations and supervised by local doctors and specialists; the school health service is operated by the municipalities. The majority of confinements take place at home, where 790 qualified midwives deliver 35 per cent of all Dutch babies.

PUBLIC HEALTH

The country's extremely high standard of public health has been brought about through years of close co-operation between the public authorities and voluntary organisations. The larger municipalities have their own public health services; elsewhere it is principally the voluntary bodies who carry out the actual work and the local authorities who promote and co-ordinate their activities. The government is chiefly concerned with the provision of medical and dental services for schools, industrial health services, environmental health and food hygiene. Particular care is taken over drinking water, especially in the light of the recent serious pollution of the Rhine, and 98 per cent of the population now receives its fresh water supplies from the central reservoirs. In future about six million people will get fluoridated water. An early warning system to detect air pollution in the industrial areas has just gone into operation at Rijnmond, near Rotterdam, and is expected to be the first of a national network.

Fortunately, the Dutch are very health and hygiene minded. The cleanliness of even the humblest snack bar and the public lavatories is outstanding. In such an overcrowded country this is immensely important. Fresh air and a balanced diet are already part of their way of life; the problem of the future is rather to see that every citizen gets adequate living space and the recreational facilities essential for the maintenance of his mental health and well-being.

Deaths from tuberculosis have decreased since the war, and new cases amount to only 40 per 100,000 persons. Vaccination, although not compulsory, has virtually eliminated smallpox, diphtheria, whooping cough and poliomyelitis. Holland has not, however, escaped the three 'killers' of the twentieth century: a marked increase in heart disease among younger people, cancer, and an increasing number of deaths from road accidents.

FOOD AND DRINK

The Dutch have the reputation of being big eaters, yet their daily consumption of calories per head of population is lower than in many other countries: Holland, 2,932; United Kingdom, 3,247; United States, 3,090.

Eating habits differ from England and America in that it is customary in Holland to take only one hot meal a day. This may be at midday in agricultural households, but is usually eaten in the early evening. It is often preceded by the traditional *borrel*, a small glass of Dutch gin (drunk neat and iced), or, for ladies, a medium sherry. The meal nearly always begins with a vegetable soup, sometimes containing meat balls or noodles. Better-class households may serve a grapefruit or prawn cocktail, or (in season) *nieuwe haring*, slightly salted raw herring with toast, but this is not everyday practice unless there are guests. Delicacies such as smoked eel are reserved for special celebrations and dinner parties. The main course is invariably meat and potatoes, with one or two vegetables (often one green vegetable and apple purée), and plenty of gravy. Meat is of excellent quality but expensive, and beefsteak at 40p ($1.04) a portion is beyond the reach of the average family, who content themselves with the cheaper cuts of beef and pork. A favourite dish is *gehaktballen* (minced meat balls). Lamb is rarely eaten, and fish—no longer compulsory on Fridays for Catholics—less than once a week. For dessert there is usually *vla*, a flavoured custard which the Dutch call *pudding*, stewed fruit and cream, pancakes or apple tart. Water or beer (mostly lager) may be drunk with the meal, wine only on special occasions.

Cheese is not normally eaten at dinner, but rather for breakfast and lunch. The basis of both these meals is bread, of which there is a variety, including delicious rye bread, eaten with different cold meats, sometimes paper-thin smoked beef, tinned fish, cheese, jams and other sweet spreads. This is washed down with tea (weak and without milk) at breakfast and usually with milky coffee, buttermilk or plain cold milk at lunch. Some families add a fried egg or croquettes to the *koffietafel*, as the midday meal is called, or in summer salad and fresh fruit. The famous *uitsmijter*, one or more fried eggs on bread with slices of cold roast beef or ham, was invented many years ago as a late night snack at the end of a party (its name literally translated means 'chucker out'); it is nowadays a popular quick lunch in snack bars and restaurants.

In general, the Dutch like plain, wholesome food at home, but expect a high standard when they eat in restaurants. They do not take kindly to being hurried over a meal and often smoke a cigarette at table between the main course and dessert, even at home.

The daily routine is punctuated by cups of tea and coffee, which are always served with a biscuit or piece of chocolate. Everything and everyone stops for the mid-morning *kopje koffie*. There is usually a cup of tea in the afternoon, and after dinner, from eighty-thirty onwards, any number of cups of one or other beverage. The older generation still keep a pot of tea hot under a huge cosy, or on a special burner, for several hours; but nowadays coffee is gaining favour. The Dutch are perfectionists over their coffee, which they drink strong with a few drops of condensed milk. Visitors are often astonished to be offered a cup that is only two-thirds full. This is the *Haagskopje*, a custom dating from the time when the higher civil servants of The Hague earned much less than the wealthy traders of Amsterdam and Rotterdam, but were envied by the latter for their high social status. The little economies practised by the Hague people were imitated, first by the Rotterdammers and Amsterdammers, and then all over the country, and since that time it has been considered impolite to pour out a full cup.

An industrial worker spends 37 per cent of his income on food, drink and tobacco, and the white collar worker about 27 per cent. Major expenditure is on meat and meat products (20 per cent), milk and cheese (15 per cent), bread (7 per cent), biscuits and cake (7 per cent), vegetables (7 per cent), fruit (7 per cent), jams and articles containing sugar (5 per cent), oils and fats, but not butter (4 per cent), potatoes (3 per cent).

As butter is expensive, equivalent to about 40p (96 US cents) per English pound, 60 per cent of the people eat only margarine. Unilever, who make two-thirds of all the margarine sold in Holland, have eight different qualities on the market, ranging from a cheap brand (mainly for cooking) at just under 5p (12 US cents) a half-pound to special 'diet' margarine at 10p (24 US cents) a half-pound. Roughly 46 pounds of margarine per head are consumed each year, as against just over $6\frac{1}{2}$ pounds of butter. The bulk of Dutch butter (one standard quality, non-salted) is therefore exported, but supply exceeds demand; the government faces a problem of the huge stockpile of unsold refrigerated butter, which periodically it sells to the home market at less than cost price.

Cooking methods are quite different from English and American. Meat, always sold boned, is rarely roasted or grilled, but is braised, stewed or fried. Potatoes are cooked very slowly in a little water until all the liquid is absorbed, then shaken in the pan until soft and flaky. Specialities of the Dutch kitchen include the

---

Hilversum town hall, built in 1931, the work of architect W. M. Dudok.

'Corporate Unity' by Wessel Couzijn, the world's largest bronze sculpture (nicknamed 'the scrap iron monument'), commissioned by Unilever NV for the pool in front of its new headquarters in Rotterdam. An example of the way Dutch industry supports the arts : each floor of the building has works of art from a different European country.

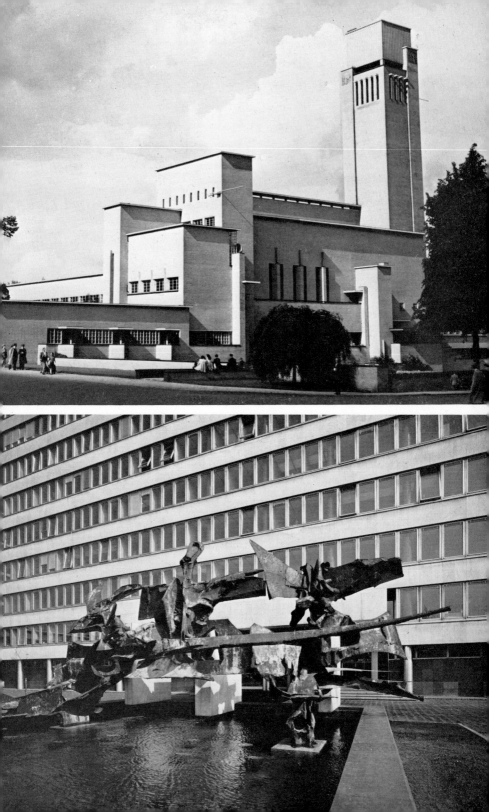

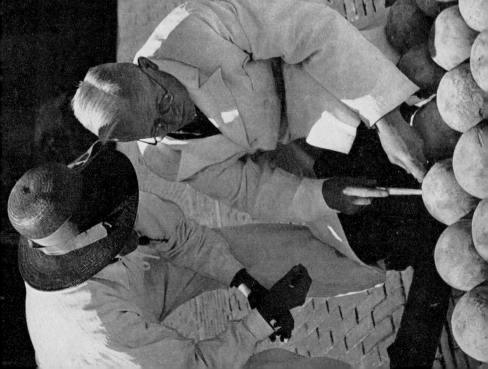

famous winter dish, *erwtensoep*, a thick pea soup with pork, bacon and sausage in it; *boerenkool met rookworst*, a hash of potatoes and kale with smoked sausage; and *hutspot*, a mixture of boiled beef, potatoes, onions and carrots, traditionally eaten in Leyden on 3 October to celebrate the anniversary of liberation from the Spaniards. Those who have lived in the Indies, and many other Dutch people, enjoy Indonesian cooking; a number of restaurants will deliver this kind of meal in hot containers to the house.

Although a Hollander may not often take his wife out to dinner, neither does he expect her to spend hours at the kitchen stove. All Dutch home cooking is geared to what is the simplest to prepare. The housewife is very spoiled : she buys her vegetables already cleaned and prepared, even baby new potatoes and mixed chopped vegetables for soup; the *vla* for dessert comes in bottles delivered by the milkman; cakes and pastries from the local confectioner. Yet frozen foods, when first marketed on a large scale in the early sixties, were slow to catch on, partly because of price and the fact that their international packaging meant smaller portions of vegetables than those to which the Dutch were accustomed, but principally because the housewife, with time on her hands, felt guilty about using them. As incomes

---

Traditional way to eat the new herring.

Inspecting the produce at Alkmaar cheese market.

rise and as more married women are tempted into employment, the pattern of consumption is expected to change.

Most women shop daily, which explains the low percentage who have refrigerators. The 'little shop round the corner' is fast disappearing: already 37 per cent of all food shops are self-service and most of the multiple stores have supermarkets. By 1975 it is forecast that 71 per cent will be self-service and that these shops will handle 90 per cent of total turnover. For the time being, at any rate, the milkman's, greengrocer's and baker's carts, which bring their commodities to the housewife's front door, remain a familiar sight, along with the colourful flower carts that are so much a part of the Dutch street scene.

SMOKING

Filter cigarettes are most popular with Dutch women, of whom 42 per cent are smokers. Among the 64 per cent of men who smoke, 48 per cent smoke non-filter cigarettes and 38 per cent cigars.

Tobacco advertising is not permitted on television, but there are no restrictions on advertisements in the press. Only recently has an anti-smoking campaign been launched in the schools.

CHANGING STANDARDS

Life in the 1970s is a strange mixture of old and new values. The rather rigid, stratified society that still dominated Holland twenty years ago is crumbling fast, and the permissiveness of the post-war generation seems more 'advanced' than in the United Kingdom.

Those who openly practise the swapping of marital partners are in the minority. But the freely available contraceptives, the drug-addicts, abortion clinics and sex shops, are visible symptoms of the immense social upheaval which the country is undergoing today.

4

How They Work

TWENTY-FIVE years ago predominantly agricultural (she was even called a 'land of farmers'), Holland has become a highly industrial state and a competitor to be reckoned with in international trade. Looking back over this remarkable transformation, it is clear that it would never have been achieved but for Marshall Aid and the hard work and co-operation of the Dutch workers during the post-war austerity years.

The war had followed hard on the heels of the depression of the thirties, and at the time of the liberation in 1945 the Dutch economy was at a very low ebb. The health and working capacity of the population was much impaired, transport non-existent, fuel and power were virtually nil. Such industrial plant or agricultural machinery as had existed before the war was obsolete or in ruins. Inflation followed, and a shortage of foreign exchange was aggravated by the loss of Indonesia. And just when economic growth was under way, there came the flood disaster of 1953.

These adversities brought out the best in the Dutch character. Massive imports, financed by foreign loans, helped to get production going and to restore the health and energy of the people. Currency reform and a capital levy backed the government's social and economic policy of thrifty living, and this was further strengthened by agreement between employers' and workers' organisations to foster industrial peace in the interests of reconstruction. From the outset everything was geared to industrialisation and the assumption that economic growth would be dependent on the close integration of Dutch industry with that of western Europe.

With the coming into force of the Benelux customs union in 1948, and the resumption of trade with West Germany in 1949, the balance of payments deficit began to decrease. Renewal of commercial relations with newly independent Indonesia in 1949 helped, and in 1952 the government announced that it no longer required Marshall Aid. In the years 1948-52 this had totalled $1,137,600,000. During the same period industrial production per worker had risen by 17 per cent.

The boom which began in 1953 and lasted until 1957 enabled Holland to withstand the cost of the 1953 flood without recourse to further foreign aid, but it was not to last indefinitely. Parallel with increased productivity the government had to house, educate and provide employment for the growing population, and by 1956 money was again becoming tight as national expenditure began once more to exceed revenue.

In January 1958 the coming into effect of the European Economic Community gave the Dutch economy a much-needed shot in the arm, boosting industrialisation and heralding the start of another boom. By 1961 it was strong enough to bear the weight of a 5 per cent revaluation of the guilder and the introduction of a 45-hour five-day week.

Industrial production rose by an average of over 6 per cent annually in the years 1955-66, the gross national product by 4.5 per cent. While this rate of growth was maintained throughout the sixties and Holland enters the seventies on a wave of even more rapid industrial and economic expansion, the country has had to face, and still faces, enormous difficulties. Since 1964 the balance of payments position has fluctuated considerably due to over-spending and a shortage of skilled labour on the one hand and unemployment on the other, culminating in the now total collapse of the government's prices and incomes policy. Theoretically, the strengthening demand for exports to EEC countries which began in 1967 and continued through 1968 and 1969, coupled with a more lively rate of investment, ought to have eased the situation; in fact, the prospects of future stability are now threatened by inflation on the domestic front, Mao-ist inspired violence and industrial unrest.

Nevertheless, with exports paying for 90 per cent of imports, and total output having trebled in the last twenty-five years, Holland has done incredibly well. The new inflation may be nothing more than a teething trouble in the implementation of the EEC tax harmonisation policy. When the transitional period is over, and provided that wages and prices can be held to a reasonable level, the balance of payments position must improve. The 1970 surplus of 2,559 million guilders reflects a substantial inflow of foreign money (2,473 million guilders net on the private capital account).

Meanwhile, in industry, in trade and shipping, and in that third mainstay of the Dutch economy, agriculture, there is a widespread outward air of prosperity. Roughly 42 per cent of the working population is now employed in industry, 51 per cent in the services sector (about half of these in trade and transport), and 7 per cent in agriculture and fisheries.

GROSS NATIONAL PRODUCT

Since 1960 the gross national product (130,210 million guilders in 1971) has been increasing at the average rate of 5.1 per cent. This works out at approximately £1,000 ($2,600) per head of population, which is now higher than the United Kingdom but still much below the United States. In the light of the advanced state of industrialisation already described, the figure seems astonishingly poor. Of the original six EEC member countries, only Italy has a lower gross national product *per capita*. The reason is simple : in Holland, as in Italy, the married woman is not, generally speaking, gainfully employed.

At the time of going to press, the results for 1972 are not available, but a 4 per cent increase over the previous year has been forecast and, for the period 1970-4, an average annual growth rate of 4.3 per cent.

THE LABOUR MARKET

The Dutch labour force, including service personnel, amounts to approximately 4.7 million, 37 per cent of the total population. Ninety per cent of the males in the 15-65 age group are gainfully employed, but less than 30 per cent of the females. Eighty per cent of the working population are wage or salary earners, the rest either self-employed or engaged in a family business.

Except in the teaching and medical professions, or where there is some pecuniary reason, it is still unusual for a Dutch married woman, with or without children, to go out to work. Traditionally the man is expected to provide, the woman to look after the house and family. The viewpoint is changing slowly, and some firms successfully operate a part-time employment scheme in order to attract female labour back to the factory bench. Less than ten years ago, however, the husband of a working wife laid himself open to raised eyebrows and a few snide remarks on the part of neighbours and colleagues.

Only about 7 per cent of married women are employed outside the home, and of these as few as 2.6 per cent work on their own account or for an employer : the majority assist in their husbands' businesses. Catholic women tend to work less after marriage than Protestants, which creates a problem in the south, forcing NV Philips' Gloeilampenfabrieken of Eindhoven to send buses daily to collect women and girls from northern Belgium, where there is a shortage of work. Comparatively few women get to the top : among approximately 250 managers and deputy managers at Philips throughout Holland, there is only one woman.

Like other European countries since the war, Holland suffers from the 'brain drain' of highly educated and trained personnel. In some ways this is less disastrous here than in the United Kingdom, for Holland is overcrowded and competition for top jobs is keen. There is, however, a very real shortage of skilled labour, for in addition to those emigrating overseas, many have been attracted by the higher wage packets to be earned in West Germany. Unskilled labour remains short in the industrialised western region, and for some years now Holland has systematically recruited foreign workers from Mediterranean countries. The foreign labour force has grown from 30,000 workers in 1958 to over 100,000 in 1972. This figure includes some 23,000 Belgians and 800 Germans who commute daily, but not the 45,000 Dutch immigrant workers from Indonesia and the colonies.

As agriculture has become more mechanised, less manpower has been needed on the land, and the government's policy of encouraging firms to develop new plant away from the over-crowded west has not yet solved the unemployment problem in parts of the northern, eastern and southern provinces. Under the supervision of the Directorate-General for Manpower, much has already been accomplished through vocational training schemes, supplementary employment for the physically or mentally disabled and for certain other categories of workers and artists, as well as the creation of new jobs in State civil engineering and public works projects.

Unemployment, which rose from 56,000 in 1970 to 96,000 in 1972, constitutes about 3.5 per cent of the current working male population and 1.5 per cent of the female working population.

LABOUR RELATIONS

Management-employee relations enjoy an excellent record in Holland, until recently one of the few countries of western Europe to have suffered scarcely any strikes since the last war.

The principle of co-operation between employers' and employees' organisations agreed on immediately after the war has been continued. The highest representative body in this field is the Social and Economic Council, whose membership is drawn from the government and the employers' and employees' organisations in equal numbers. The council acts in an advisory capacity to the government on all socio-economic matters. Another body, chiefly concerned with wages policy and the co-ordination of the various labour organisations, whose advice is also sought by the government from time to time, is the Joint Industrial Labour Council, on which the employers' and employees' organisations, although not equal in numbers, have a parity of vote.

Every firm with more than twenty-five employees is obliged by law to establish a works council for the mutual discussion of all relevant problems.

Whereas the trade union movement developed in Holland towards the end of the nineteenth century, the formation of employers into organisations did not become general until after World War I. There are now four federations existing side by side and independently of each other, to which most of the numerous industrial, trade and agricultural employers' organisations are affiliated: the Federation of Netherlands Employers and the Central Social Employers' Federation, which are non-denominational, the Federation of Protestant Employers' Associations and the Roman Catholic Federation of Employers' Associations. Roughly 30 to 40 per cent of all trading firms belong to one of these associations; in industry, membership is almost 90 per cent, in agriculture 70 per cent.

Trade unionism revived immediately after the war, but has never been compulsory: less than half the working population are active union members. A communist-inspired movement to unite all workers in one body soon petered out, and after some regrouping three major federations emerged: the Netherlands Federation of Trade Unions (NVV), which had existed before the war; and two denominational federations, the Netherlands Federation of Catholic Trade Unions (NKV) and the National Federation of Christian Trade Unions (CNV). The NVV, with a membership of 611,401 in 1971 (36 per cent of union membership in the whole country) is the largest: twenty unions are affiliated. The NKV claims almost 28 per cent (401,802 members), the CNV, 15 per cent (238,330 members). Some 319,400 workers belong to non-federated unions, among them a declining communist union.

SALARIES AND WAGES

In the twelve months following the disintegration of the government prices and incomes policy in 1963, earnings rose twice as fast as during the previous ten years. The fifteen-year-long struggle to hold them to a level linked with productivity had utterly failed. The final straw was the shortage of labour which, having placed employees in a strong bargaining position, must be held largely to blame for the wage explosion that resulted : a 16 per cent rise in 1963, 11 per cent in 1964, 13.6 per cent in 1965. Thereafter wages have continued to spiral at an average rate of 12.5 per cent, well above that of productivity. By October 1972 the average gross pay of most Dutch workers was 130 per cent higher than the 1962 level.

The 1963-5 rise was of course exceptional. Over the last two years the gross wage of an adult industrial worker has risen by approximately 25 per cent, the cost of living price index by 20 per cent. At the beginning of 1972 the average gross wage of an agricultural worker was £28 ($67) a week, that of an industrial worker £34 ($88). Assuming that the latter was a married man with two children under the age of sixteen, his 'take home' pay (gross wage plus children's and holiday allowances, less deductions for social security and tax) amounted to just over £27 ($70). (The holiday allowance, to which all State employees and most others have been entitled by law since 1966, is now 6 per cent of their total annual remuneration, including overtime and bonuses. It is paid in a lump sum, usually in May.) A guaranteed minimum weekly wage for adult workers in full employment was introduced in January 1966. This is currently just over £22 ($57).

Practically all salaries and wages are negotiated on a collective basis by the employers' and employees' organisations, subject to government approval. An employer is not free to fix the remuneration of his staff; before 1963 some employers were guilty of paying 'black' wages above the legal maximum in order to attract labour. Except for the clergy, domestic labour and a few private categories which are not controlled, there is a separate collective agreement (CAO) for each work group. Agreements are revised annually, and the new CAOs come into force on 1 April, fixing the rates of pay and conditions of employment for the ensuing year. They are immensely complicated, for the wage structure takes into account not only the grade and age of the employee, but also in some cases the municipality in which he works. Many CAOs provide for equal pay for equal work. The rights of women in this respect have been generally recognised only in the last five years but have not yet been universally applied for fear of the cost to the economy.

Working hours vary from forty hours a week for office and bank staff to forty-five hours in industry. Shop personnel normally work a forty-two-hour week, with either one full day or two half days off a week and five free Saturdays in the year. Some overtime is worked, especially in branches of the transport industry, where a forty-nine to fifty-four-hour week is quite common. Increased mechanisation has gone a long way in recent years towards bringing the agricultural workers' hours into line with those of industry.

Some fairly typical *gross* annual salaries drawn from the various occupational groups are:

Shop assistant	£1,200 ($3,100)
Shorthand-typist/ secretary	£1,500-£2,500 ($3,900-$6,500)
Primary school teacher	£3,000 ($7,800)
Commercial traveller	£3,500 ($9,000)
Secondary school teacher	£3,500-£5,000 ($9,000-$13,000)
Company director, doctor or dentist	£7,000 ($18,200) upwards

Money continues to depreciate at a steady annual rate of around 3 per cent. A guilder is currently worth rather less than was 70 cents ten years ago. Wages having in the meantime risen by approximately 5 per cent more than consumer prices, the Dutch worker is now slightly better off. The 'moderately applied' wage and prices freeze introduced in 1971 was lifted in August 1972.

WORKERS' INSURANCE

The provisions of the social security scheme have been outlined in the previous chapter. Special legislation, however, relates to the Dutch worker: the Health Insurance Act, guaranteeing a sickness benefit of 80 per cent of his wages (up to a maximum daily rate) for fifty-two weeks; the Working Incapacity Act, providing the same benefit where incapacity lasts for more than fifty-two weeks, with a sliding scale according to disability; the Unemployment Benefits Act, under which the unemployed or redundant are entitled to 80 per cent of their normal daily wage for up to twenty-six weeks a year; the Wage Earners' Children's Allowances Act and the Self-Employed Persons' Children's Allowances Act, providing a fixed allowance for the first two children of a wage earner or a lower income self-employed person.

Contributions are based on a percentage of income, with a fixed maximum to be paid by the employer and employee together. They differ in various branches of industry, but the average percentages are:

	Employer	Employee
Health Insurance Act	6.3	1.0
Working Incapacity Act (WAO)	4.05	1.35
Unemployment Benefits Act	0.5	0.5
Wage Earners' Children's Allowances Act	3.3	–

The cost of the children's allowances paid to the lower income self-employed person is borne by the government; no contributions are levied in this respect.

Factories employing more than 750 workers are obliged to run their own industrial medical service.

THE PROFESSIONS

The professional person occupies an honoured place in Dutch society. Long years of study pave the way to a successful career, for great store is set by professional qualifications and each group has a strictly observed hierarchy and a rigid code of etiquette.

Medicine, the law and civil engineering used to be the most popular; the modern trend is towards the social sciences. There is no distinction as in the United Kingdom between a barrister and a solicitor: a *meester in de rechten* in private practice functions as a lawyer and may plead in court. He is addressed as *meester* ('Mr' in writing); an *ingenieur* (engineer) puts 'Ir' in front of his name; the holder of a *doctorandus* (master of sciences) degree 'Drs'. The telephone directory lists a person's profession alongside his name and address.

AGRICULTURE AND FISHERIES

Gone are the days when Holland boasted an equal number of cows and people : the ratio is now one to two. The problem of the post-war era—how to feed the growing population on less than half an acre of farmland per person—has been overcome by mechanisation and high productivity arising out of co-operative farming.

The agricultural labour force is now half what it was in 1950, but output has increased to the extent that 50 per cent of all Dutch produce (25 per cent of the country's total exports) is marketed abroad. On top of the 7 per cent who earn their living from farming, market gardening or fishing, about a quarter of the working population does some job connected with it, either in processing or distribution. The number of farmers' sons and daughters who work on their parents' farms is high, and only 15 per cent of the 154,000 farms and 38,000 horticultural holdings employ regular hired labour.

Farms are small by British and American standards; many still only 25 acres. Roughly 48 per cent are owner-occupied. Rents average £12 ($31) for farms, while detached arable and grass land is approximately £8 ($20) an acre.

Land is precious and is therefore worked intensively. Much of the soil is sandy, requiring more fertiliser per acre than is used in any other European country. For this reason, the modern tendency is to concentrate on high-yield horticultural products, pigs and table poultry, and to import grain, which can be produced more cheaply elsewhere. Potatoes, cereals and sugar-beet are nevertheless grown in considerable quantities.

Land consolidation is high on the list of government priorities. As old farms become vacant, or when farmers can be transferred to new holdings such as those on the IJsselmeer polders, land is bought up, improved through irrigation and drainage, and re-parcelled so that it may be used to best advantage. Many old farms consist of several isolated strips of land. Government aid to farmers takes various forms; subsidies of 30 to 40 per cent on new farms, the provision of agricultural education and research facilities, veterinary and plant protection services.

Within the Common Market, Holland must fall into line with other member countries. At Brussels in recent years Dutch delegates have exerted considerable influence, and the originator of a joint EEC agricultural policy, Dr Sicco Mansholt, a former Dutch Minister of Agriculture and now president of the European Commission, believes the 200-acre farm to be the economic minimum for Europe.

Livestock and dairy produce

Although more than half the farming land is under grass, Holland suffers from a shortage of fresh fodder for her livestock, and care is taken to import concentrates of high nutritional value. Kept primarily for dairy purposes, black and white Frisian cattle are a familiar sight all over Holland, but especially in the northern provinces. Friesland and Groningen have a worldwide reputation for cattle- and horse-breeding.

Even where the process is mechanised, milking takes place mainly in the fields, except during the winter months, which is said to be one reason why the Dutch cow gives the highest milk yield in the world. Sixty per cent of total milk production is sold on the home market, in liquid or dairy product form, the remainder being processed into export butter, cheese and condensed milk. Farmers are finding specialisation to be the only way of keeping prices down and quality high; many now supply wholesalers with poultry, calves and pigs on a contract basis. A large proportion of the four thousand million eggs produced annually is exported.

Horticulture

Rising living standards in Western Europe have created a demand for high quality vegetables, and hothouse lettuces, cucumbers and tomatoes from Holland now fill the shopping baskets of housewives in many countries all the year round. The 'Westland', a triangular area between the Hook of Holland, Rotterdam and The Hague, where most of these are grown (and also grapes, melons and flowers), is known as 'the kitchen garden of Europe.' Some 7,500 acres are under glass. In other parts of the country large quantities of vegetables, especially early potatoes, are grown out of doors. The surplus fruit crop from the Betuwe and Limburg orchards is mostly canned or made into jam.

So important are flowers and flower bulbs to the national economy that more than 10 per cent of the total agricultural land is devoted to their cultivation. Government and industry-sponsored research ensures that the tulip, hyacinth, daffodil and, more recently, the lily bulbs sent all over the world (North America being the biggest customer) are good growers and virus-free. The proximity of the Aalsmeer flower market to Schiphol enables flowers to be flown to their destination within a short time of being auctioned. The Dutch system of auction is unique : the 'clock' starts at a high figure, and buyers must use their judgment in pressing the button on the counter in front of them as the hand moves to a lower price. Business is booming, and many farmers and horticulturists are finding it more profitable to switch from other crops to flowers.

Since only 7 per cent of the country is forest and woodland, forestry plays a very small role in the Dutch economy. The government has, however, planted extensive forests in the province of Drente.

Fisheries

Considering the extent of Holland's North Sea coastline, the fishing industry plays a relatively unimportant role in the economy. Most of the annual catch of 300,000 tons, about 40 per cent of which is herring, is sold for export or processing.

The herring industry developed in the late fourteenth century, when a fisherman called Willem Beukelszoon discovered how to cure the fish. It is now an important international trade, with Germany, Belgium and France the principal buyers of fresh, salted and pickled herring. Only in Holland are the young herring eaten almost raw (very slightly salted), although many visitors who succeed in mastering their initial nausea become great addicts of this delicacy. Every spring the opening of the season is fêted and there is a race to bring the first catch back to port; traditionally the first barrel of new herring is offered to the Queen.

While North Sea trawlers land huge quantities of herring, haddock and cod, the inshore fishermen bring in mainly plaice, sole, turbot and brill. The Delta project has necessitated the removal of the famous Zeeland oyster and mussel beds to the Waddenzee and Lauwerszee region. For the mussels, 80 per cent of which are sold to Belgium and France, the transition has been effected without detriment, but the oysters are settling less happily in the colder and more tidal northern waters.

Up to forty years ago sea fishing was the main occupation in the ports along the Zuyder Zee. Even when this became the freshwater IJsselmeer, many still earned a good livelihood from its abundant stock of eel and perch. As more and more land has been reclaimed, however, the fisherfolk have been pushed out to the North Sea coast and their sons and grandsons into farming or industry. Exceptionally, the inhabitants of Urk, once an island and now a flourishing fishing port due to its new position on the south-west tip of the North-east polder, have profited. In the 'costume' villages of Marken and Volendam, so beloved of tourists, they must now rely more than ever on revenue from glossy picture postcards, dolls and gaily painted wooden clogs. In Zeeland there is the same problem, and for those who are too old to be retrained, it means not only a complete break with family tradition but in many cases enforced retirement at the State's expense.

FUEL AND POWER

The most exciting development of this century has been the discovery of vast untapped fields of natural gas in the north of Holland. Commercial production on a large scale started in 1963, and resources are now estimated at 77,000 thousand million cubic feet. Sales have doubled each year since 1966, reaching about 486 thousand million cubic feet in 1968, of which 69

Aalsmeer flower auction, where buyers bid 'against the clock.'

Dutch tomatoes grown in the Westland are exported all over western Europe.

per cent was for internal consumption (industrial and domestic) and 31 per cent was exported to Germany, Belgium and France. It is planned to extract about 1,050 thousand million cubic feet a year, half of which will be exported through a network of pipelines that is being extended year by year. By 1975 over a third of Holland's own energy requirements should be met by natural gas.

Another big stimulant for industry in 1968 was the first supply of nuclear energy produced by the 54 MW capacity Dodewaard nuclear power station. Much research is being carried out in the nuclear field, both at the national and international level, with financial assistance from the government. Since January 1968 Holland has participated in a consortium with West Germany and Belgium for this purpose. She has also entered into an agreement with the United Kingdom and West Germany to share the costs of a pilot scheme to produce cheap nuclear energy, using the ultra-centrifugal method invented by the Dutch nuclear scientist, Professor Jacob Kistemaker. Although there is an abundance of water, the fall of the rivers is so slight as to have little value as a source of hydro-electric power, and at present the bulk of the country's fuel and power is derived from gas and oil. Coal used to be the most important, and the south Limburg

---

The main building of Leyden University, the oldest in Holland, founded by William of Orange in 1575 in gratitude for the town's resistance to the Spaniards.

Lecture in progress at the Aula Technische Hogeschool, Delft.

mines (four State-owned, eight privately controlled) are among the most modern in Europe. Competition from natural gas and petroleum, and also from cheaper imported coal, has resulted in the gradual running down of the industry; it has recently been announced that the State coal mines are to close completely by 1975.

Several oilfields have been developed in Holland since the war, but their crude oil output (over 2 million metric tons in 1968) meets only about a quarter of the country's needs. Rotterdam handles a rapidly increasing traffic in oil exports and imports. Among the five major oil companies with refineries in the Rotterdam-Europoort complex, the Shell installation at Pernis, with its newly extended capacity of 25 million tons, is the largest in the world. Total refining capacity at Rotterdam exceeds 60 million tons.

The exploration and production of oil and natural gas are carried out by *NV Nederlandse Aardolie Maatschappij* (NAM), in which Shell and Esso have an equal interest; the crude oil is transported to their refineries near Rotterdam for processing. Distribution of natural gas is handled by *NV Nederlandse Gasunie*, whose shares are held by the Dutch government (10 per cent), the State mines (40 per cent), Shell and Esso (25 per cent each).

Although the United Kingdom started drilling in the North Sea as early as 1964, concessions for drilling in Dutch territorial waters were not granted by the government until 1968. Since that time a significant oil strike has been made some 50 miles north of Vlieland by a four-company consortium headed by Tenneco, and an important natural gas strike north-west of Den Helder by the NAM group.

Electricity power stations are combined in a national grid, which is connected to the Belgian and German grids. Production in 1970 totalled 40,859 million kilowatt hours, of which almost 26,400 million were used in industry and trade, 8,600 million in private domestic consumption.

INDUSTRY

Two of the world's biggest industrial concerns outside the United States have headquarters on Dutch soil. The Royal Dutch/Shell group is 60 per cent Dutch, 40 per cent British. Unilever, originally a combination of the *Margarine Unie* (van den Bergh's and Jurgens) of Holland and Lever Brothers of Great Britain, has two parent companies, Unilever NV of Rotterdam and Unilever Limited of London, controlling 500 subsidiary companies in 70 countries. Philips, a firm of purely Dutch origin, whose name has become a household word in almost every country in the world, ranks eighth on the list of largest companies of the Common Market. These three giants today employ between them, in Holland alone, about 2.75 per cent of the working population (world employment figures are in brackets): Philips, 99,000 (367,000); Royal Dutch/Shell, 18,650 (185,000); Unilever, 19,000 (324,000).

Dutch government policy has always been to interfere as little as possible in trade and industry, rather to give full scope to private enterprise while at the same time creating a favourable industrial climate through training and research and by providing incentives for investment. In very few cases has the government given direct financial assistance to industry: the only State-run concerns are the post office, the mint, the government printing and publishing works, the State mines, the gas industry, the fishing harbour at IJmuiden, and the manufacture of artillery equipment.

Industry has existed here in a small way since the early seventeenth century. Holland then led the world in shipbuilding, a trade which Peter the Great of Russia came specially to Zaandam to learn. Compensated for the lack of natural resources by a favourable position for the importation of raw materials, shipbuilding led first to mechanical engineering and the metal manufacturing industries and then to textiles, and agriculture to the development of a food and drink industry. Heavy industry began after World War I, but has developed on a large scale only since 1945. The last ten years have been characterised by a veritable explosion in the field of scientific and industrial research and by a growing trend among companies to merge.

The following table gives a rough breakdown of how the working population is employed in the major sectors of industry today:

Building	26	per cent	
Metals and machinery	13.6	,,	,,
Food and luxury articles	12	,,	,,
Transportation	8.3	,,	,,
Clothing and cleaning	6.8	,,	,,
Electrical	6.2	,,	,,
Textiles	5.6	,,	,,
Chemicals	4.7	,,	,,
Mining	2.7	,,	,,
Other industries	14.1	,,	,,

100

It is hardly surprising that building heads this list. The immediate post-war priorities were the reconstruction of Rotterdam and other devastated towns and the vast new housing programme. Since then there has been no slackening in the demand for industrial plant, schools, hospitals and research centres on the one hand, and roads, bridges, dykes and dams on the other.

Among the metal manufacturing industries, one of the world's most modern steelworks is the *Koninklijke Nederlandsche Hoogovens en Staalfabrieken NV*, known familiarly as 'Hoogovens' (meaning 'blast furnaces'). The forthcoming merger of Hoogovens with Hoesch of Germany will enable a giant steelworks to be built for the 1980s. The new company, as Europe's third largest steelmaker, is expected to have an annual output of eleven million tons.

In the field of non-ferrous metals the newest development is the aluminium works at Delfzijl, opened in 1966 and the first plant in the country to be powered entirely by natural gas. There are also a number of foundries specialising in ships' propellers and church bells.

Salt is found in the east and north-east of the country in quantities estimated to be sufficient to meet world demands for the next hundred years. Dutch table salt is exported all over the world, while much industrial salt is consumed by the huge soda factory at Delfzijl.

Under the heading of transportation special mention must be made of Fokker aircraft and DAF motor vehicles. The Fokker Friendship (F-27) has proved to be the biggest seller in commercial aircraft since the war, and the Fokker Fellowship (F-28) looks like being equally successful. There is a special version, the F-228, for the American market. Fokker recently merged with the German firm, VFW, and the new company is to participate in the European A300B airbus project.

Well known for their commercial motor vehicles, *van Doorne's Automobiel Fabrieken* of Eindhoven has achieved great success with private cars and now lies fourth in the sales figures for Holland. Locomotives, railway wagons and trams are mainly imported, but buses, bicycles and mopeds also come off Dutch assembly lines in steadily increasing numbers each year.

About three-quarters of Holland's shipbuilding production is sold abroad, from passenger liners to tugs, barges to yachts. There is also a big demand these days for floating dry docks, derricks and all types of oil drilling equipment, which the Dutch claim to have supplied to almost every area of the world's oceans where offshore drilling takes place.

Gerard Philips produced his first electric light bulbs at Eindhoven in 1891, with a staff of ten. Four years later, his younger brother Anton entered the company. Today their firm has national organisations in sixty countries of the world and production plants in forty of them, with a turnover (1971) of 18,120 million guilders. Light bulbs are still manufactured (40,000 different types nowadays), along with all manner of household appliances, radio and TV sets, X-ray apparatus, components, electronic equipment, gramophone records, computers, video tape recorders and—newest of all—air pollution monitoring equipment. Fully equipped hospitals and schools are supplied to developing countries.

There are Philips factories in various parts of the country. Eindhoven, where 38,000 are employed is dominated by the 'light tower,' so called because light bulbs are tested in the building day and night, and by the dome of the 'Evoluon,' a permanent exhibition on the evolution of man, civilisation and the development of technology in the service of mankind, founded in 1966 in celebration of the seventy-fifth anniversary of Philips.

The most spectacular post-war growth has been in chemicals, which followed naturally in the wake of the massive expansion of the oil refining industry. Firms not primarily concerned with chemicals, such as 'Hoogovens,' Shell, Unilever, the State mines and Philips, have entered this field. Some two thousand products are now manufactured, ranging from fertilisers, disinfectants and paint to cosmetics and medicines, all of which find a ready market in the EEC. Soaps and detergents constitute 20 per cent of Unilever NV's annual turnover.

Two of the 'top ten' Dutch industries, *Algemene Kunstzijde Unie NV*, which combines chemical and salt production with that of artificial silk and other synthetic fabrics, and *Koninklijke Zout-Organon NV*, which produces salt and chemicals, merged at the end of 1969 to form a new giant known by its initials AKZO.

The manufacture of textiles and the ready-to-wear clothing industry meets about 90 per cent of Holland's domestic needs. Stores like De Bijenkorf, Vroom en Dreesmann, and C & A (which is a Dutch company, not British as many Londoners believe) sell a range of clothes which bring high European fashion within the pocket of everyone. Amsterdam has a huge clothing centre much patronised by foreign buyers in the trade.

The food and drink industry is traditionally of great importance to the Dutch economy. Condensed milk, butter and cheese head the food export list, and the government exercises strict control over all dairy foods (no cheese may be exported unless it bears the official stamp). Unilever, in addition to margarine, make many other edible products, and also deep frozen foods. The industry includes the canning of fruit and vegetables, jam manufacture, meat and fish products, soft drinks and a vast range of biscuits and confectionery. Holland ranks second among the world exporters of beer, brewed mainly from imported hops. Dutch gin and liqueurs are world-famous, and so is chocolate—some 150 million pounds of bar chocolate or chocolate articles are marketed every year.

Imported tobacco is manufactured into about 2,000 million cigars and nearly 20,000 million cigarettes a year. Amsterdam still enjoys a high reputation in the diamond trade, but this has declined considerably since the war. The industry used to rely almost exclusively on Jewish labour, but so many Jews lost their lives during the war that it has been difficult to revive the diamond-cutting trade. Nowadays only about five hundred people do this delicate precision work. Other important industries are paper and printing, with many books printed in Holland for British and other publishers, leather goods, timber and furniture, glass and ceramics, silver and pewter.

The government spends a good deal of money on attracting foreign visitors to Holland, and although receipts from tourism have rocketed from £23 million ($55 million) in 1954 to £176 million ($422 million) in 1970, Dutch people travelling in other countries now spend more than the total receipts from tourism at home.

The Utrecht Trade Fair, held in spring and autumn, and other specialised fairs throughout the year attract exhibitors and buyers from all over the world. The completion of a world trade centre, now being built in Amsterdam on the lines of those of New York and Tokyo, is scheduled for 1975. A similar giant centre is planned in Rotterdam.

SHIPPING AND TRADE

As long ago as the seventeenth century the Hollanders had earned themselves a reputation as 'carriers of the oceans.' Today vessels flying the Dutch tricolour (horizontal stripes of red, white and blue) trade in almost every sizeable port throughout the world. The Dutch ports alone handle over 200 million tons of goods a year. At least 60 per cent of the craft which ply regularly up and down the Rhine laden with goods to and from the European hinterland are registered in Holland; in 1970 this traffic reached a record of over 112 million tons, made possible by the development of 'pusher-boat' navigation, one boat pushing a string of barges.

Despite her geographical position, Holland might never have become the major shipping nation of Europe but for the man-made waterways linking Amsterdam and Rotterdam to the sea. The North Sea Canal, opened in 1876, made Amsterdam the world's only tide-free harbour, with direct access for the largest ocean-going vessels of the day. Having cut a deep channel through the IJ lake and then through a 12-mile stretch of lowland to the coast, at the point where the modern port of IJmuiden now stands on the south bank and 'Hoogovens' on the north, the engineers drained the lake on either side of the new canal and turned it into farmland. Less than a hundred years later that same land is now being re-converted in order to provide deep water harbour facilities for the growing number of cargo and container ships using the port.

Access to Germany and Switzerland has been much improved by the Amsterdam-Rhine Canal, suitable for vessels of up to 2,000 tons, which was opened in 1952. The Tiel lock, where the canal joins the river, is one of the largest inland navigation locks in the world.

Rotterdam's artificial link with the sea, the New Waterway, was opened to shipping in 1872. The brain-child of a young Dutch engineer, Pieter Caland, this 20-mile-long channel, entirely free of locks and bridges, was considered at the time to be much too 'daring.' It was to prove its worth within thirty years, for when the German Ruhr burst into frenzied industrial activity at the turn of the century it was through this waterway that the bulk of the increased traffic passed. Even during the economic crisis of the thirties the tonnage handled by the port continued to increase, until by 1938 Rotterdam vied with London for second place among the world ports.

In 1945, harbour and city were in ruins. Reconstruction was started immediately, and a plan which had been worked out in secret during the German occupation—to construct an inland harbour basin in the stretch of water between two branches of the Meuse known as the Botlek, and to turn the land flanking it into factory sites—was put into operation in 1947. It was to add 3,200 acres to the port area. A few years later the Botlek Plan was enlarged in order to accommodate the tankers and refineries of an expanding oil industry. Within an incredibly short time of starting again from scratch, Rotterdam first overtook London and later New York to become the busiest—if not then quite the largest—world port.

The decision to embark on the construction of Rotterdam-Europoort, an 9,000-acre complex of harbour, industrial and storage facilities near the mouth of the New Waterway, opposite the Hook of Holland, was taken in 1957. Work on this 'gateway to Europe' (*poort* means 'gateway') is proceeding at such a rate that statistics, no sooner given, are out of date. Two-thirds of the cost, estimated at over £100 million ($240 million) is to be met by the government, one-third by the municipality of Rotterdam. Initially the approach channel was deepened so that the largest ships afloat could enter the port through a temporary entrance. Super tankers with capacities of up to 225,000 tons already use the permanent entrance, and by 1974 one of these tankers is expected to berth every other day. A hundred million tons of oil will flow through the port of Rotterdam annually.

Reclamation of the *Maasvlakte*, a notoriously treacherous sandbank close to the shore, will provide an additional 6,500 acres now being developed as harbourage for these giant vessels, backed up by what the Dutch call 'front door' industrial sites. A plan to create similar industrial areas in the adjoining Delta region is under consideration. Meanwhile Rotterdam is already the largest ore trans-shipment port of Europe and, thanks to the new grain terminal in the Botlek, the leading continental grain port. For general cargo purposes roll on/roll off facilities and two container centres equipped with container cranes are fully operative. Total handling capacity amounts to 10,000 tons an hour. In 1970, 31,867 ships berthed at Rotterdam, landing cargo of approximately 165 million tons; total cargoes handled by the port exceeded 225 million tons.

By 1974, the target date for completion of the new harbour entrance, Rotterdam-Europoort (total area 25,000 acres which includes the Botlek and Maasvlakte, the various basins for sea-going and inland shipping, and the container basin) will be the world's largest, safest and most accessible port. Schiedam, Vlaardingen and Maassluis form part of the Rotterdam complex; other busy Dutch ports are Zaandam, Harlingen, IJmuiden, Dordrecht, Flushing and Terneuzen. In April 1970 the government sanctioned the construction of a new passenger ship and container harbour between the Hook of Holland and Maassluis. Many of the vessels serving the smaller ports are coasters designed for both sea and inland navigation, which makes trans-shipment unnecessary.

The government normally bears the cost of maintaining the approaches to the Dutch seaports, most of which are municipally owned. Local authorities are responsible for the construction and maintenance of harbour facilities, but not for the day-to-day operation of the ports, which is left to private enterprise. Amsterdam and Rotterdam have their own port authorities.

BANKING

Banking has flourished in Holland since the seventeenth century. Then it financed trade and shipping; today it is concerned mainly with industry.

De Nederlandse Bank is the central authority. Banker to the government for years, it was nationalised in 1948. The Bank has special responsibility for supervision of the credit system. Buying on hire purchase is nowhere near as prevalent here as in Britain or America, but it is gaining in popularity as costs rise.

Several important mergers have taken place recently among the commercial banks, most of which are private limited companies. The *Algemene Bank Nederland*, a merger of the

Twentsche Bank and the *Nederlandsche Handelmaatschappij*, and the *Amsterdam-Rotterdam Bank*, popularly called 'AMRO,' a combination of the *Amsterdamsche Bank* and the *Rotterdamsche Bank*, together handle about 60 per cent of the country's commercial banking business.

There are also agricultural credit banks affiliated to central co-operative banks which meet the credit requirements of agriculture and trade, 250 independent savings banks and about 30 mortgage banks. The *Nationale Investerings Bank* furnishes risk-bearing capital to small enterprises that would not normally have access to the capital market. The municipalities have their own *Bank voor Nederlandse Gemeenten* which grants credits out of funds obtained on the capital market against the issue of debentures.

In Holland the private individual does not use his bank account as the Englishman does. For the payment of bills he normally uses his 'giro.' Almost every individual and firm has a 'giro' account. The Dutchman who puts money in the bank expects to get interest on it, whether it is in a current account, on which the present rate is $2\frac{1}{2}$ per cent, a deposit account or a savings account, where interest varies according to the notice of withdrawal specified. In the last two years the banks have issued customers with *betaalcheques* valid up to a certain sum, which they may use to purchase goods in the shops or to settle household bills.

EXPORTS AND IMPORTS

Trade between Holland and the Belgo-Luxembourg Economic Union (BLEU) has increased steadily since 1948, when import duties were abolished between the three countries and a common tariff agreed for imports from other countries. Benelux is now the world's fourth largest trading power, after the United States, the United Kingdom and West Germany; its domestic market alone numbers 22.5 million consumers.

Membership of the Common Market has also greatly stimulated Dutch exports and imports. Its most significant effect has been to concentrate trade within the community: beween the years 1958 and 1968, EEC imports into Holland rose from 41.9 to 55 per cent, and Dutch exports to EEC countries from 41.6 to 57 per cent. The challenge of foreign competition which faced Dutch enterprises following the demolition of EEC internal tariffs is fast being overcome through rationalisation, increased efficiency and the fashion for mergers and takeovers. Many companies have strengthened their position by associating with foreign concerns, and in recent years there has been quite an influx of American and British companies and subsidiaries.

The current trade pattern is one of steady growth on all fronts, with the increase perhaps most marked in the flow of goods to and from West Germany. In 1970 Dutch exports totalled 42,622 million guilders and imports 48,603 million guilders. Trade with other west European countries accounted for approximately 71 per cent of Dutch imports and 82 per cent of exports, and with the United States for 10 per cent of imports and 4 per cent of exports. Seven per cent of Dutch exports went to the United Kingdom, whose goods made up 6 per cent of imports into Holland. Within Europe the following breakdown of these figures is significant:

	Imports	Exports
	per cent	
West Germany	27	33
BLEU	17	14
France	8	10
Italy	4	5
EEC countries (total)	56	62
EFTA countries (total)	11	15
Other European countries	4	5
	71	82

Half of every guilder in a Dutchman's pocket today has been earned by exports.

5

How They Learn

FORMER Minister of Education Joseph Cals once said that the Netherlands had many schools but no school system. This is far from true today. Thanks largely to the strenuous efforts of Mr Cals, legislation has been enacted in the past fifteen years, much of it only after a long and stormy passage through parliament, that has revolutionised the education of the Dutch child.

The most far-reaching of these changes came into effect as recently as August 1968, so that it is really too soon to judge how far they have been successful. These were embodied in an Act concerning all post-primary education other than at university level, devised by an earlier Minister of Education, Professor Rutten, but brought (and fought) before parliament under Mr Cals' ministry, which ended in 1965. The field it covered was so wide, and the changes envisaged so enormous, that the Dutch, with their fondness for nicknames, could not resist dubbing it the '*Mammoetwet*' ('Mammoth Law'). Practically overnight Mr Cals became a sitting target for the cartoonists, who mostly chose to depict him as a diminutive elephant-boy leading an elephant-like monster. Preparation for the change-over took two years, yet teachers, parents and pupils still remain bewildered by it all. Controversy over the new Act is one of the major talking points in Holland today.

The constitution is specific as regards education. The relevant chapter begins : 'Education shall be an object of constant solicitude on the part of the government . . .' and goes on to lay down

the principles upon which the educational system has long rested
—that all compulsory education shall be free, that every person's
religious beliefs shall be respected, and that parents shall have
freedom of choice concerning their children's schooling.

In practice this means that both public and private schools
receive State finance and that any denominational group or
other voluntary body has the right to establish its own school.
There are altogether nearly 19,000 educational institutions in the
country. The public schools are fully maintained by the State,
the private schools run by religious or other groups are subsidised
by the government. While the majority of private schools are
Roman Catholic or Protestant, there are a number of Jewish
schools and some based on the Dalton or Montessori teaching
methods; the non-denominational private schools are, however,
relatively few.

The Minister of Education and Sciences has overall responsibility for educational legislation and the enforcement of the
relevant Acts, except in the case of agricultural education, which
falls to the Minister of Agriculture. The school syllabus is under
the supervision of government-appointed school inspectors, who
are directly responsible to the Inspector General of Education.
The minister is advised by two bodies appointed by the Crown—
the Educational Council and the Academic Council. Every
school is obliged by law to conform to a certain standard of
teaching and to final examination requirements. State schools
must give pupils the opportunity of religious instruction if their
parents so wish. In all other respects the various educational
establishments enjoy considerable freedom of action, since in the
absence of any central authority they are answerable only to
their own school board or to their local council.

About 70 per cent of all Dutch children attend private schools,
and the remaining 30 per cent go to State schools. With the
exception of a few girls' schools, all are co-educational. The
English custom of sending middle- and upper-class children to
boarding school does not exist in Holland, unless there are special
family circumstances or where a child is mentally retarded or has
a physical or psychological problem which needs special care.

For such children there are special schools in the various grades—nursery, primary and secondary.

The law on compulsory education has been amended several times since its introduction in 1900. At present every child is obliged to attend school for a minimum of eight years. In 1969 a Bill was passed through parliament raising the compulsory term of education to nine years, which it has not yet been possible to put into effect owing to the shortage of school accommodation. A child must now attend primary school at the age of seven, which means that he may leave when he is fifteen; he may, however, start school at six (and most children do), so that he is entitled to leave when he is fourteen.

Between the years 1958 and 1968 the number of pupils receiving full-time education rose from two and a half to just over three million. It is growing annually with the increase in population and also as more young people take advantage of the opportunities for higher education and vocational training. When the school leaving age is raised a sharp increase is expected the following year; by 1980 the forecast is 3,720,000 and by the year 2000, around 5,050,000.

The school day normally begins at 8.30. Except for nursery and primary school pupils, most Dutch schoolchildren attend classes on Saturday mornings, but this is changing. The long holiday falls earlier than in the United Kingdom, running from the beginning of July to the middle of August. This is shorter than the summer vacation enjoyed by American children, who do not, however, get the full two weeks at Christmas and at Easter normal in Holland. When Easter falls late, the Dutch schools usually close for two or three days at the beginning of March for what are called 'crocus' holidays. There is also an autumn holiday of one week around 20 October.

Three of the four new Acts envisaged under the radical overhaul of the Dutch educational system are already in force: the Pre-Primary Education Act, which became effective in 1956; the Scientific Education Act* in 1961; and the 'mammoth' Secondary Education Act in 1968. The fourth, a new Primary

* 'Scientific' in this context means 'university.'

Education Act was recently approved by parliament. Transformation from the old system to the new must take place gradually, as year by year the old grades disappear. For the moment, the two systems run parallel to a certain extent, as may be seen from the following outline of the various school categories.

Corporal punishment is illegal in Holland.

NURSERY SCHOOL

Kleuteronderwijs, or nursery school education, is not compulsory in Holland, although in fact about ninety per cent of all children attend this type of school for one or two years. A child may be admited from the age of four, but must leave when he is seven. The education is virtually free, parents contributing less than £1 ($2.60) per child each month.

There are two sessions a day (8.30 to 11.30 and 2.30 to 4.30) on Mondays, Tuesdays, Thursdays and Fridays, and on Wednesdays from 8.30 to 11.30 only. Tuition follows a co-ordinated plan of work and play, and includes physical exercises and games.

Over a quarter of a million children attend nursery school.

———

Amsterdam: school class learning about Rembrandt's 'Night Watch' at the Rijksmuseum; posting a letter on the back of a tram delivers it to the head Post Office within minutes

Out of over 6,000 schools, about 75 per cent are privately run (2,281 Roman Catholic, 1,946 Protestant and 545 administered by voluntary bodies). These private schools are financed largely by the municipalities, which are reimbursed by the government, while the public infant schools are administered by the municipality and fully maintained by the State. In 1969 the cost of keeping a child at nursery school for one year worked out at approximately £70 ($182).

PRIMARY SCHOOL

The long-awaited new Primary Education Act, which replaces the old one of 1920, embodies an entirely new concept in basic education.

Whereas the former system, with its minimum standard of achievement for all pupils, aimed at providing a complete general education for those who would not go on to secondary school, the emphasis now is not on a minimum standard, but on the individual aptitude of the child. The class system, under which a pupil who did not reach the specified standard had to repeat a year, has been scrapped. The division of the curriculum into

———

The new Schiphol airport, 13½ft below sea level and ready to receive the 'jumbo jets.'

The container terminal at Rotterdam.

subjects is restricted, and teaching is now orientated towards the following groups: language (including English), writing and arithmetic; history, geography, biology, physics, hygiene and road safety; handicrafts, music and art; physical education, including swimming.

This new-style primary education is intended to be a foundation for subsequent secondary education and not complete in itself. The former VGLO and ULO schools for extended primary education have ceased to exist, and all primary schoolchildren now go on to one of the three grades of secondary school. The advanced primary school leaving certificate, which used to be the standard recognised by all Dutch employers, has been replaced by the MAVO (secondary modern) final examination—roughly the equivalent of O-levels in the United Kingdom.

The school time-table normally runs from 8.45 to 11.45 in the morning, with a fifteen-minute break, and from 1.30 to 3.45 in the afternoon.

There are at present about 8,200 schools, staffed by 46,000 teachers, catering for the educational needs of 1,428,000 children between the ages of six and sixteen. Public and private schools are on the same financial footing: school building and material operating costs are borne by the municipality, teachers' salaries by the State. In the case of private schools, the municipality must spend the same amount per pupil as it does on public primary education. In 1969 the total overhead cost per primary school child came to just over £100 ($240).

SECONDARY EDUCATION

Under the new Act, entrance examinations for admission to secondary school have been abolished in favour of psychological tests or trial classes, the choice being at the discretion of each individual school. Another innovation is the 'transitional' class, which gives students the opportunity to adapt to their new school and to determine their future course during the first year of pre-university education rather than at the outset. The old uniform programme of secondary education, dating from 1876, has been replaced by one in which pupils in the higher classes may make their own choice of subjects for which they will eventually take an examination. There are of course certain subjects which are compulsory.

Secondary education falls into four categories: pre-university, general secondary education, vocational training, and other forms of secondary education. The timetable is much the same in the various schools: a minimum thirty lessons each week in the first, second and third classes, and thirty-two in the fourth, fifth and sixth classes. The amount of homework varies from school to school and may involve anything from two to four hours' study. Classes begin at 8.30 or 8.40. There are usually four lesson periods of fifty minutes each during the morning session, with a ten-minute break, and three similar lessons in the afternoon. Most children take sandwiches to eat at break and lunchtime, and nearly all schools set aside a special room where pupils may eat their *boterhammen*, or picnic lunch. If they wish, all school-children may get milk, for which parents pay 75 per cent, the balance being made up by the municipalities and dairy producers. Meals at school are provided only for those needing special care; they are paid for by the parents.

Pre-university education

The three types of school in this category (known as VWO), the *gymnasium*, the *atheneum* and the *lyceum*, all run six-year courses and prepare students for entrance either to university or to other institutes of higher education.

Under the old system, the only pre-university school was the *gymnasium*. Latin and Greek predominated, and students were able to split into an 'A' stream, with emphasis on classical languages, or a 'B' stream, mainly mathematics and science, only in the last two years of their course. In the new style *gymnasium* they divide into 'A' and 'B' streams from the third year onwards. New subjects such as social and political science and handicrafts have been added to the curriculum.

Classical languages do not figure in the general syllabus of the *atheneum*, or modern grammar school, which is taking over the role of the former *hogereburgerschool* in so far as the HBS prepared students for higher educational studies. Nowadays, in the last three years, students split into an 'A' stream, specialising in economics and social sciences, or a 'B' stream which concentrates on mathematics and the natural sciences. Latin may be added as an optional subject.

The *lyceum* is a combination of *gymnasium* and *atheneum*. Like the other two, it features a 'transitional' year and provision for private study periods. All *lyceum* students, however, take a uniform basic course in their first year. They have the advantage of being able to switch to another type of education later on if their first choice should not prove to be the right one.

The new scheme is well under way, and the former style *gymnasium* will have ceased to exist by 1975, the HBS by 1974.

General secondary education

Those who do not intend to go on to university may be admitted to one of three grades of general secondary school—HAVO, MAVO or LAVO—higher, middle or lower *algemeen voortgezet onderwijs*.

The HAVO, or higher grade schools, are gradually replacing the former HBS which, founded in 1863 by the great statesman, Johan Rudolf Thorbecke, were intended originally to provide a sound education for those who would not go to university but would make their career in industry, trade or commerce. Students take a five-year course, for the last two of which they may choose four optional subjects in addition to the compulsory Dutch and one modern language required for the final examination. In the first year at HAVO, tuition covers the same subjects as in the new transitional class at the *gymnasium* or *atheneum*. The leaving certificate qualifies the student for admission to higher vocational training, but not to university.

The MAVO four-year course corresponds to that given at the former ULO schools, providing what might be called either a secondary modern or advanced primary training. A separate three-year course may also be taken. As with the HAVO final examination, Dutch and one modern language are compulsory and the student may choose four other subjects. The old type of ULO school will disappear by about 1972.

The LAVO schools are intended to fill the needs of the broad masses after the age of twelve by providing a general education as given formally by the VGLO schools. Primary school pupils may transfer to a LAVO school for a two-year course, or may incorporate this in their first two years at a lower vocational training establishment. Most of the VGLO schools have now been transformed into LAVO schools or other schools which come into the vocational training category.

Vocational training

Vocational training in Holland falls into eight branches, in most of which tuition is given at elementary, intermediate and higher levels. These comprise technical schools and those specialising in agriculture, home economics, trade, commercial and clerical training, socio-pedagogy, teacher training, arts and crafts. Courses mostly last for three or four years, the requirement for admission being, in the lower grade, a six- or seven-year primary education; in the middle grade, a three-year MAVO certificate; in the higher grade, depending on the course, either a four-year MAVO, a HAVO or a VWO certificate. One very important feature of the new Act is that technical school pupils showing sufficient aptitude are now able to go on to university.

Another form of vocational training is the apprenticeship system, which has developed strongly in recent years. This is carefully regulated by the Apprenticeship Act, under which a boy or girl, in addition to being properly trained in the trade or craft, must attend school four evenings in the week or one full day in the week. Daytime attendance is rapidly gaining in popularity.

Unless young people are under apprenticeship, they may not take up employment before their fourteenth birthday. Those who work from the age of fourteen are encouraged to attend classes at educational establishments catering especially for their needs. Some of the big industrial concerns run their own voluntary educational and training schemes. Philips, for instance, not only has its own international institute for post-academic studies in electronics, to which students come from all over the world, but also a technical school which runs a three- to four-year course for boys from the age of fourteen. Classes in foreign languages and administration are available to staff members.

HIGHER EDUCATION

Holland has six universities and seven institutes at university level. There are also a number of *hogescholen*, institutes of learning on the same level but which are not called universities because they have either fewer than three faculties or none in medicine, mathematics and physics.

Leyden, Groningen and Utrecht have State universities, and Amsterdam a municipal university. There are also two private universities—the Free (Dutch Reformed) University of Amsterdam and the Catholic University of Nijmegen. The three technological institutes at Delft, Eindhoven and Enschede count as State universities, as does the agricultural university of Wageninen. Privately-run institutes at university level are the Catholic school of economics at Tilburg and the non-denominational school of economics at Rotterdam. There is to be a State university at Rotterdam, where there are already faculties of law, sociology and medicine.

With the passing of the Scientific Education Act, which became effective in 1961, the universities achieved a greater independence than hitherto, allowing for internal reorganisation and more co-operation between the various institutions. New financial measures were introduced at the same time, putting public and private universities on an equal footing. The government now subsidises the private university institutes for 100 per cent of their net expenditure.

Anyone who pays necessary enrolment fees may attend a Dutch university, whether or not he wishes to sit for the examinations. Degree candidates need a pre-university school certificate. Before the war university students were drawn almost exclusively from among the upper classes and from abroad, but nowadays there is a cross-section of all the social strata. Scholarships or interest-free loans to cover maintenance, books, etc are available for those whose families are in the lower income bracket. The average length of a university course is six years, culminating in a doctorandus degree. In the law faculty it is five, in medicine (the most overcrowded), seven or eight years. As they are not obliged to sit examinations, students who are not inclined to work, but whose parents can afford to support them, often stay at university for much longer.

University tuition fees are to be raised from £25 to £125 ($325) a year in the near future, and an entirely new system of grants will be introduced.

Most young men and women studying at university belong to one of the several student societies (denominational or otherwise) which cater for a variety of cultural activities. There are separate societies for male and female students. Young men with wealthy parents behind them usually join a student *corps*, which involves attendance at beer drinking sessions similar to those at German universities (but not the duelling). Every five years a *Lustrum*, or festival, is held at the beginning of the university year, with three days devoted to theatre, cabaret, parties and balls. Since there are no halls of residence within the universities, most students also become members of an organisation which entitles them to eat cheaply at student cafés.

Opportunities for specialist training in the professions are manifold. There are schools for librarians and archivists, senior nursing staff, social workers, film makers, journalists, and many more. Special mention must be made of the music *conservatoires*, of which there are two in Amsterdam and one each in The Hague, Rotterdam, Utrecht, Tilburg, Maastricht and Groningen.

ADULT EDUCATION

Largely in the hands of private associations and extra-mural organisations, and subsidised by the government, adult education is gaining in importance as people have more leisure. Broadly speaking, it takes three forms: day or evening classes and short-term courses; public libraries; amateur cultural activities.

For professional people and those changing their careers in middle life, qualifying examinations are of great significance. Unlike in Britain and America, almost everyone who wishes to open a business in Holland must hold the necessary diploma (estate agents, for example). Another factor is that as people are promoted they need new skills. Language classes are very popular.

TEACHER TRAINING

It is expected that by the year 2000 there will be more people employed in education than in agriculture. How the number of teachers is likely to increase is shown in the following table:

Teachers (x 1,000)	1964	1980	2000
infant school	13.1	18.1	22.0
primary school	48.1	60.0	78.0
secondary school	59.0	95.0	135.0
university	21.0	42.0	95.0
Pupils per teacher			
infant school	34	30	30
primary school	30	25	25
secondary school	16	16	16
university	3	3	3
Teachers as a percentage of the working population	3.2	4.2	5.4

The above figures are taken from 'Education and manpower forecasts' by R. Ruiter, in *Planning and Development in the Netherlands*, III, 1/2, 1969.

A full course at teacher training college lasts five years and is divided into three parts: the first, for those who have not had a VWO education; the second, teacher training proper, leading to a teacher's certificate; and the third, training for headmaster- or headmistress-ships. Students who complete the third part of the course successfully may study psychology and pedagogics at university level.

Special arrangements apply to teacher training in technical, agricultural and horticultural schools. Until quite recently this was possible only at evening school, but there is now a school in Rotterdam giving a one-year residential course in technical teacher training. Most secondary agricultural and horticultural schools hold teacher training classes for those who wish to take their diploma in those subjects.

Dutch teachers are civil servants. Their salaries are therefore based on a fixed scale according to their grade, age and length of service. By British standards they are very good indeed. (The secondary school teacher with a university degree is on the same level as an army officer or a higher grade civil servant.) Certainly you do not encounter among the teaching profession in Holland the mounting dissatisfaction as to conditions and pay now prevalent among teachers in Britain; nor is there any shortage of recruits to the profession.

Student unrest, on the other hand, erupted in May and June 1968 over the Maris Report which suggested a more centralised administration of the universities, and the report was finally rejected. In June 1969 two hundred students occupied the administrative centre of Amsterdam University. Other demonstrations followed, but there was little violence. At one stage seventy-five artists occupied the room in the Rijksmuseum which houses the famous 'Night Watch' painted by Rembrandt, demanding a voice in State cultural policy.

In the 1972 budget estimates 10,553 million guilders (23.5 per cent of all State expenditure) have been allocated to education. Of this about 20 per cent will be spent on higher education.

6

How They Get About

GETTING about a country as small and flat as Holland presents few problems. Thanks to an extensive modern network of communications and a highly efficient public transport system, for the traveller it is one of the most comfortable of all western European countries. The difficulties lie rather with the engineers who must contend with the presence of water only a few feet below the land surface (at least in the western half of the country) whenever new roads, bridges, tunnels or—as very recently— underground railways are planned. It is a tribute to their skill that it is possible easily to travel the entire length or breadth of the land within a few hours.

Whatever the method of transport—car, or more sedate bicycle or canal barge—traffic is normally kept moving in an orderly way. On summer Sundays and at the peak holiday periods it is true that there are often huge snarl-ups on roads to the popular resorts—but where nowadays does this not occur? At least the everyday rush hour in the towns and industrial areas is shorter and public transport seems less congested than elsewhere, due to the Dutch dislike of commuting long distances and to the thousands whose favourite means of travelling to and from their work is still by bicycle.

There are eight million bicycles in Holland today, which means that virtually everyone between the age of six and sixty has one. Although the design has been streamlined slightly in the last few years, Dutch bicycles still look old-fashioned to British eyes, being solidly built with high saddles and handlebars—but as anyone who has ever attempted to ride a lightweight model here on a windy day soon discovers, they are immensely practical. About two-thirds are home-manufactured, the rest imported mainly from Common Market countries.

Perhaps on account of their superiority in numbers (the ratio of bicycles to private cars is 3 : 1), cyclists tend to behave as though they ruled the road. It can be a motorist's nightmare to drive through an industrial area just after the factories have closed for the day. Most major roads have cycle paths, but in the towns cyclists weave in and out of other traffic in an alarmingly carefree way. It is not uncommon to see two sweethearts cycling gaily along the busy streets hand in hand, or a middle-aged gentleman riding dangerously near to the middle of the road, one hand on the handlebar and the other supporting a huge black umbrella against the rain. Another hazard is the housewife who goes shopping by bicycle—and wobbles home laden with one basket strapped on to the back and a second swinging from the handlebar. In the days immediately after the war when bicycles were scarce (it was necessary to have a permit to obtain one), the habit grew of giving friends a lift on the back, and for a long time this practice was winked at by the traffic police. It is still permitted but not much seen except in the outlying country districts.

At least the bicycle is silent. This cannot be said of the *brom-fiets*, or motorised bicycle, which has become such a craze in the last twenty years and whose constant drone, resembling a high-pitched road drill, now eclipses all other street sounds. In 1970 there were 2 million of these noisy mopeds on the road, as well as 65,000 motor cycles and scooters.

The private car explosion in Holland dates from the early sixties, when the first-fruits of post-war industrialisation began to be harvested. In the previous decade the number of vehicles registered had risen by 20-30,000 annually, but in 1961 the number shot up from 522,000 to 615,000 within twelve months and has been spiralling ever since. At a total of 2.5 million in 1971, this averaged one car per 5 inhabitants, as compared with one per 4.7 in the United Kingdom, one per 2.3 in the

United States. Few Dutch families own more than one car. It is forecast that by 1975 there will be as many as 2,875,000 cars in the country.

Only 7 per cent of private cars on the road are of Dutch manufacture. The automatic DAF, and a later model called the Daffodil, scornfully dubbed 'the housewife's car' by the male population, are said to have tempted thousands of women into the driver's seat. For the rest, over 37 per cent are German (the Volkswagen and Opel are especially popular), 29 per cent French, 6 per cent British and about 7 per cent Italian. Among the others are a rather small number of American models and— quite recently—some Japanese cars.

The Dutchman who bought a new car in 1971 spent on average just under £1,000 ($2,600). Total sales for that year show that of all new cars purchased only 6 per cent cost under £600 ($1,560), 66 per cent were in the £600-£1,000 ($1,560- 2,600) price range, and 28 per cent over £1,000. There used to be a roaring import trade in secondhand cars, totalling about 60,000 a year, mainly from West Germany, but since 1969 import regulations aimed at cutting down the number of these cars on the road have succeeded in reducing this figure by about a third.

Holland suffers badly from 'Sunday drivers.' Many people, it seems, keep a car for weekends and holidays but rely on their bicycle, their own two feet or public transport (in that order) for every day. The reverse also applies, for many a Monday to Friday motorist abandons his car in favour of the bicycle for Sunday recreation—but in diminishing numbers. Out of the yearly average of 11,250 miles driven per private car, only 1,375 miles relate to the journey between the home and place of work.

In spite of a severe driving test, both practical and written, the general standard is not spectacularly high. The Dutch motorist drives fast on the motorways but exasperatingly slowly in town, well under the 30 mph speed limit. Since he is not blessed with the quick reactions of the Frenchman or Italian, and the traffic lights change directly from red to green, he rarely seems to get away smartly from a stationary position. Very occasionally you encounter the Dutch driver in a hurry—usually the opulent type who sits hunched behind the wheel with a fat cigar in his mouth—who will sound his horn, flash his lights and cut in at the slightest opportunity until he has a clear road.

The improvement of interurban communications, coupled with the increase in the number of private cars, means that far more people move around the country more often than they did twenty years ago. It is estimated that an average of just over 4,000 miles are travelled annually per head of the population, compared with approximately 1,250 miles in 1948. (This in spite of the fact that few Dutch workers commute for more than three-quarters of an hour.)

Leaving aside those who walk or cycle, for whom statistics are not available, the way the majority travel is broken down as follows:

Private car	66	per cent
Bus	12	,, ,,
Moped	11	,, ,,
Train	9	,, ,,
Motor cycle	1	,, ,,
Tram	1	,, ,,
	100	

In future these percentages will have to be slightly adjusted as a proportion of bus and tram travellers change over to the new metro systems planned for Rotterdam and Amsterdam. The first metro line (in Rotterdam, opened 1968) already carries 90-100,000 passengers on a normal working day.

RAILWAYS

Since before World War II the running of the Dutch railways has been in the hands of one company, *NV Nederlandsche Spoorwegen*, in which the State is sole shareholder. Out of the total network of 1,968 miles, 1,029 miles are already electrified, and trains are not only fast and comfortable—they are also punctual, well-heated and (which cannot be said of all European trains) **clean.**

Passenger transport accounts for 54.4 per cent of revenue, and an average of half a million travellers per day is carried. As more people acquire private cars, however, regular passenger traffic slowly declines. Freight, providing 40.1 per cent of the railways' income, has been hit by keen competition from road and inland waterway transport firms, with the result that the *Spoorwegen* have not shown a profit since 1964. The worst year on record was 1967, when the deficit amounted to 94 million guilders (£10,800,000; $25,920,000); this was reduced to just over 80 million in 1968. Inclusive rail holidays, international car-sleeper trains (almost 10,000 cars were carried by the Dutch railways in 1969) and special holiday trains like the *Bergland Expres* to Austria, Switzerland and Italy and the *Zonexpres* to the south of France, Italy and Spain are helping to some extent to offset this loss, and a new factor has been the growing popularity of 'mini trips' during the off-peak season. On the freight side, a subsidiary company, *Van Gend en Loos*, once renowned for its fine horses (it was the last to abandon horse-drawn transport just after World War II), handles the collection and delivery of goods by road in conjunction with the railways. Passenger luggage and mail make up the balance of the *Spoorwegen* revenue.

In 1968 the Dutch railways blossomed in new garb—bright yellow paint and a new symbol. Express services were improved; there are now four trains per hour between Amsterdam and Utrecht, three between Rotterdam, The Hague and Utrecht and between Utrecht and Arnhem, and from seven to nine trains a day between Amsterdam and Groningen or Leeuwarden. Present rolling stock consists of 673 locomotives, 1,899 passenger coaches and 19,156 freight trucks. Railway staff totals approximately 27,600.

Fares have gone up with the cost of living, but are nowhere near the highest in Europe; there are many cheap day and week-end concessions. People over the age of sixty-five may buy a card costing fifty guilders which entitles them to travel half-price on the railways inside Holland for a year. The most luxurious form of rail travel, and well worth the supplementary fare, is by one of the international Trans Europe Express (TEE) trains which link the principal cities of western Europe. By TEE, an Amsterdam business executive can be in Paris within approximately five hours, or Brussels within two-and-a-half, of leaving his office.

Holland also participates in the 'TEEM' system of fast international freight trains and in international container transport by Trans-Europe Road-Rail Express (TERRE).

METRO

When the word 'metro' was first mentioned, many Dutch people were sceptical. The difficulties were obvious, the cost astronomical. But the planners and engineers were determined, and in February 1968 Holland's first *stadspoor* was opened in Rotterdam. Running north to south, and linking the two banks of the New Meuse, the metro line has seven stations and is 3 miles 1,142 yards long. Trains run partly underground and through a 570yd tunnel under the river, partly along a viaduct above traffic level. The metro took just over seven years to build, considerably disrupting the city's traffic movements in the process, and cost £25 million ($67 million). An extension is planned to the south-west, as well as an east-west line to link the new town being built on the Alexander polder with the city centre.

Amsterdam is also one day to have a metro. Three lines are planned, and the work will take thirty to thirty five years at an estimated cost of nearly £300 million ($720 million).

WATER TRANSPORT

Passenger sea transport has decreased in the last twenty years as air travel facilities have come to the fore. Nevertheless, in spite of fierce competition, the Holland America Line has managed to hold its own on the North Atlantic route.

The ferries that were once such a feature of travel through

Holland are fast disappearing as new dams and bridges are constructed. Inhabitants of the old-world village of Giethoorn in the province of Overijssel, which has canals but no streets, move around by boat only because there is no other means of transport. Elsewhere the waterways are regarded primarily as of importance for trade and secondarily for touristic and recreational use. The best and most popular way of seeing the elegant canals and beautiful seventeenth-century houses of Amsterdam, the façades of which have been retained even where rebuilding has taken place, is by glass-domed boat, with a multilingual hostess to explain the points of interest. Those who like to get away from the pressures of modern life can board a Rhine steamer or pilot their own boat along the 3,340 miles of navigable inland waterways, of which 2,653 miles are canals.

The growth of the ports of Rotterdam and Amsterdam and the importance of inland water transport to the Dutch economy were mentioned in Chapter 4. On 1 January 1971 the Dutch merchant fleet consisted of 1,017 vessels (including 14 passenger ships and 98 tankers), with a total of 3,955,000 gross registered tons, not counting tugs and contractors' equipment.

Skating on the frozen canals.

Sailing in Friesland.

AIR

KLM, the Dutch national airline, has come a long way since its first flight from Amsterdam to London in May 1920 and the days of the two greatest names in Dutch aviation history, Albert Plesman, KLM's founder, and the pioneer airman and aircraft designer, Anthony G. Fokker. The oldest airline in the world still operating under its original name, and today one of the largest in terms of revenue ton-miles (the number of tons, passenger and freight, carried per mile over the total network in a year, which gives a more accurate picture than the actual number of passengers on journeys that vary in distance), the company celebrated its fiftieth anniversary in 1969. Its fifty-five aircraft now fly along world routes totalling 186,000 miles and cover a hundred cities in sixty-nine countries; there are seventeen KLM flights across the Atlantic every day of the year, sixty in the high season.

The Dutch are rightly proud of their airline: a record total of 2,942,000 passengers plus 128 million kgs of freight and 4 million kgs of mail carried during the year ended April 1971 pushed up the airline's operating revenue to over 1,000 million

———

In this Amsterdam bar glasses are filled to the brim, and drinkers must bend over to take the first sip of *genever* ('old' or 'young,' according to taste) from the counter.

Cigar production at NV Willem II Sigarenfabrieken, Valkenswaard.

K

guilders. That the average KLM passenger flies twice the distance flown by the average 'world' passenger speaks for itself.

About 15,000 people are employed by KLM. Half the company's shares are owned by the Dutch government, but the airline, a public limited liability company, is administered as a private enterprise. Its shares have recently been listed on the stock exchanges of Brussels and Frankfurt, and it is the only European airline to be listed on the New York stock exchange.

To meet the forecast of three to four times the present number of air travellers and about nine times the current volume of freight by 1980, KLM has, with financial support from the government, purchased seven Boeing 747B 'jumbo jet' aircraft during 1971. Six McDonnel Douglas DC-10-30s are on order for 1972-3 and, following the cancellation of the 2707 supersonic airliner project, the company has taken an option on another six DC-10s. In the meantime more DC-8 and DC-9 aircraft will be added to the present fleet, which consists mainly of DC-8s, Super DC-8s, DC-9s and one Fokker F-27.

The new Schiphol airport, built alongside the old one and opened in the spring of 1967, is being expanded to accommodate traffic up to the year 2000. It is well on the way to ousting London as the premier airport of Europe. Zestienhoven, just north of Rotterdam, is intended primarily to handle the growing Rotterdam-London traffic and charter flights to southern Europe; it also provides a useful alternative landing ground for inter-continental traffic bound for Schiphol. The two airports are linked by 37 miles of motorway.

Domestic air services between Amsterdam and the northern, eastern and southern provinces were inaugurated in August 1966 and are operated by a wholly KLM-owned company, the *Nederlandse Luchtvaart Maatschappij* (NLM) using Fokker F-27s. Another KLM subsidiary, the *Noordzee Helikopters NV*, runs a helicopter service between the mainland and the North Sea drilling rigs. The popularity of charter travel, both for passengers and freight, is reflected in the growth of two young Dutch companies, *Martinair Holland* and *Transavia Holland NV*.

All airline pilots are trained at the government civil flying school. Holland is the only country in Europe in which flight training has been under government control since 1946.

ROAD TRANSPORT

You will never see a cruising taxi in Holland. There are taxi ranks at the main railway stations and airports, and at a few busy centres in the larger towns, but normal practice is to telephone for a radio-controlled car. Tariffs vary according to the locality, Rotterdam taxis being the most expensive.

The most-used method of public transport is the bus. Not many years ago it used to be the tram, but modern buses have largely replaced the trams on inter-urban routes and in some towns. Nowadays more than 600 million passengers travel by bus and about 250 million by tram each year, compared with the 180 million who are carried by the railways.

Passenger bus services are operated by fifty regional bus companies, each licensed to cover a particular area. These companies co-operate to provide certain inter-urban services and usually have their terminus at the main railway station of the region, thus providing a good connection for rail travellers.

The British double-decker is unknown in Holland. The squat Dutch buses move easily among the dense traffic; newer models have automatic doors and ticket dispensers. Trams, which run chiefly in Amsterdam, Rotterdam and The Hague, are being similarly streamlined. Standing is not limited as in Britain, and both buses and trams usually take as many passengers as can be crammed inside. Men seem to give up their seats to older women far more than is now customary in England. Cards valid for eight journeys may be purchased at tobacconists'; they are slightly less expensive than the sixty cents (6p or 15 US cents) charged for a single journey when a ticket is bought on the bus or tram. Fares differ slightly from one town to another, but except on inter-urban services there is a standard rate per journey irrespective of the distance travelled. In The Hague a card for eight single journeys costs 3 guilders (35p or 90 US cents) and a similar card, but with the right to make a second journey within an hour (the popular *overstapje*) costs 3.60 guilders. *Overstapjes* are intended primarily for those who need to change buses or trams (they are valid on both), but the thrifty Dutch often manage to go into town and back again within the hour on the same ticket (the time of boarding the first tram or bus is stamped on the card). In Amsterdam the quaint custom is preserved of attaching a letterbox to the backs of trams. It is a splendid system, for all trams terminate at the Central Station and the head post office is near by.

Goods traffic has increased by 150 per cent in the last twenty years, and over 290 million tons of freight were carried in Holland during 1969. The latest statistics show that 335,000 commercial vehicles are registered in the country and almost 70 per cent of all EEC goods transported by road is handled by Dutch carriers.

Inter-urban and long distance traffic is carried on the excellent motorways which are nearly all linked to the international network of 'E' highways. About 470 miles of motorway have been completed and are in use; more are under construction. The total road network measures some 46,000 miles.

Already the planners are talking in terms of elevated roads to meet future traffic demands. The latest national road plan is based largely on a survey of the possible inter-urban highway network for the year 2000, produced by the Government Physical Planning Service as part of its *Second Memorandum on Physical Planning in the Netherlands, 1966*. Basically, the entire country is covered by a series of road plans, which are reviewed every ten years. The national road plan, embodying the primary lines of communication for through traffic, is financed by the national road fund, which in turn obtains its revenue partly from the State and partly from a surcharge on the vehicle road tax. The secondary and lesser road plans are the responsibility of the provinces, who receive an annual grant under the Road Costs Apportionment Act. In the municipalities, work on the ring roads and by-passes, and important cross-water communications such as the recent Brienenoord bridge and the Benelux tunnel near Rotterdam, qualify for government subsidies.

Under the National Road Plan 1968, some 1,200 miles of new roads are to be laid down during the next ten to fifteen years, and 440 miles of existing roads are to be made into motorways. By 1980 it is expected that Holland will possess almost 1,250 miles of motorway.

An excellent road system does not always make for safety. The Dutch road accident rate is higher than that of the United Kingdom or the United States but considerably lower than in Italy, West Germany and neighbouring Belgium. There is a unique alarm system operated round the clock by the Royal Dutch Touring Club (ANWB) at their emergency centre in The Hague. An SOS call sets in motion a system of repatriation and assistance for injured or stranded persons and their vehicles, wherever they may be in Europe; by special arrangement with the TV and radio companies, calls are put out to contact members after the daily news bulletins.

Like the AA in Britain, the ANWB maintains a countrywide patrol service, the *Wegenwacht*. It also advises the government and local authorities on matters concerning roads and bridges, road safety and the positioning of traffic signs. These ANWB signs are, incidentally, the clearest on the continent. In 1965 the ANWB took the initiative in establishing the European Road Information Centre (ERIC), in which the motoring organisations of the major western European countries collaborate to make weather and road conditions instantly available. About 52.5 per cent of all car owners in Holland are members of ANWB.

TRAFFIC AND PARKING

Since 1960 motorised traffic generally has increased by 140 per cent, private cars have increased by 207 per cent. It was calculated that in 1970 there were 51 cars per kilometre of road.

Not surprisingly, car parking facilities have been unable to keep pace. The situation is being remedied rather late in the day and will not be anything like adequate for some time. At present there are multi-storey, underground and roof car parks in only about a dozen town centres. No-parking zones and parking meters, carrying a fine of 15 guilders for unauthorised parking or excess stay, have helped to ease congestion in Amsterdam, The Hague, Rotterdam and Utrecht and will inevitably spread to other towns. Every available space is used alongside the canals, and fewer cars than one might expect end up in the water. A number of municipalities have completely closed their shopping centres to motor vehicles, and traffic is kept moving round the perimeter by a system of one-way streets.

The peak traffic periods run from 7.30 to 9 in the morning and from 5 to 6 in the evening. At lunch time there is no problem, since the majority of workers do not go home. Traffic police, sometimes policewomen, cope with the rush at busy intersections, and there are rarely any major jams. Older schoolchildren help to man the pedestrian crossings near the schools. The worst traffic build-up of the week usually starts early on a Sunday evening, especially in the summer, when the great rush back to town after a day out inevitably ends in a slow convoy, fractious children and exhausted parents.

Few townsfolk are able to garage their cars at night, but some of the modern luxury apartment blocks are being built with integrated basement garages or car ports. In the towns, most residential streets are already lined on both sides with cars parked bumper to bumper. Where, one wonders if the prognosis for 1975 becomes a reality, are the additional 875,000 vehicles going to be accommodated? Or, as the popular Dutch entertainer Wim Kan put it, 'How do I lose weight and where do I leave my car?', now quite a catchword and quoted in the ANWB publicity brochure.

The answer to that one, as to most of the problems facing this tightly-packed little country on the verge of bursting at the seams, must lie on the drawing boards of those who are now drafting a blueprint of Holland of the twenty-first century.

7

How They Amuse Themselves

A SURVEY of leisure activities carried out in 1955-6 showed that most Dutch people spent 66 per cent of their spare time at home, one-third of which was devoted to drinking tea and coffee and talking. Today they have more leisure hours, but the way in which they spend them is virtually unchanged. Only 25 per cent of all leisure hours are given to active recreation, 6 per cent to public entertainment and sporting events.

When the five-day week was introduced a few years ago and it became necessary to work extra time each day, most Dutch workers chose to curtail their lunch break or start work a quarter of an hour earlier rather than make up the time at the end of the day. Between 5 and 6pm on a weekday the streets are thronged with homeward-bound workers. By six they are deserted : the long evening, almost a ritual in Dutch family life, has begun.

The family usually eats as soon as the breadwinner arrives home. For those who are going out there is plenty of time to dine at home, as concerts and the theatre do not start until 8, the cinema often as late as 9.15; from 8.30 onwards is the accepted hour for informal visiting. If they are staying in, they will spend the evening reading the paper, watching television, playing bridge or chess, or just sitting and talking.

Inside and outside the home, leisure is very much a family concern. The Saturday afternoon shopping expedition is almost as sacred as the Sunday outing. The great week-end exodus from the towns, British style, has not yet caught on in Holland, although the lucky ones with second houses now tend to depart on

Saturday morning and return on Sunday night. For the rest, distances are small and the Sunday day trip is one of the high spots of the week.

The average Dutchman has no club life in the English sense, though there are, of course, the military clubs. The *Sociëteit De Witte* in The Hague, frequented by ambassadors and retired business tycoons who meet to discuss politics and the stock market, is the nearest equivalent to the Englishman's club—but it is unique. When a Dutchman speaks of his 'club,' he generally means some professional or trade association, sports club, political or religious organisation, or a group connected with his pet hobby, whose lectures and excursions he attends. Sixty-five per cent of the male and 45 per cent of the female population belong to one or more such society. The upper- or middle-class housewife usually belongs to a group of bridge- or tennis-playing friends or to one of the countrywide women's clubs similar to the British Women's Institutes.

Organised leisure appeals more to the younger generation, most of whom belong to one of the sports clubs, a youth club or a denominational movement. A comparatively new development is that of district and village community centres catering for a wide variety of cultural and physical activities for all age groups.

Everyone who works has a paid holiday. Most workers get a minimum of three weeks plus the official public holidays (New Year's Day, Easter Day, Ascension Day, Whit Monday, Christmas Day and Boxing Day), with extra days for long service. Civil servants' leave is based on salary scale and age. The Queen's birthday (30 April) is a national holiday for the civil service and most industrial workers, but Good Friday is not a general holiday except in the civil service. The anniversary of the liberation on 5 May 1945 is celebrated as a national holiday every five years.

Increased prosperity and the growing popularity of package tours and charter flights has put foreign travel within the means of thousands of working-class people. Between 1960 and 1966 the number of holidaymakers going abroad almost doubled. Statistics are confusing, since some people now afford a second holiday, but in 1970 out of the 46 per cent of the population who took a holiday, 3.7 million spent it in Holland and 2.9 million went abroad.

Most of those who stay in their own country choose seaside, camping and caravan holidays either along the North Sea coast or in the Veluwe and Limburg regions inland. The younger generation sometimes spend part of the summer in organised camps or on cycling or walking tours.

The quest for sunshine is universal, and most travellers head south. About 67 per cent take their own cars, which makes statistics difficult to obtain since they usually visit more than one country. Spain, Italy and Yugoslavia are high on the list for package tours, while motorists tend to visit West Germany, France, Belgium and Luxembourg in large numbers. Austria and Switzerland are popular for summer and winter holidays, and a high percentage of white-collar workers and professional people now take a second holiday at winter sports or one of the many off-season four-day trips to Paris or London. Less than 2 per cent go outside Europe for their annual holiday.

SPORT

Sport has come to play an important role in Dutch life only within the last sixty years, as a result of shorter working hours and the encouragement of Church and State. Except for swimming and the compulsory two hours' physical exercises or gymnastics once a week, with a qualified instructor, sport does not figure in the school timetable as it does in England. Athletics and team games are an after-school activity, taught in the various sports clubs to which most boys and girls belong.

Twenty per cent of the population now actively participate in some form of organised sport, compared with a mere 0.6 per cent in 1900, and the 15,000 clubs throughout the country, representing forty-one different sports, boast a total membership of more than two million. The largest—the Royal Netherlands Football Union—has over 600,000 members.

Most spectator sports take place on a Sunday afternoon, but

in the strictly Protestant districts always on a Saturday. The national sports are soccer (which the Dutch call *voetbal*), cycling, and—to a lesser degree—skating and swimming. Up to ten years ago professionalism existed only in boxing and cycling, but nowadays most of the top soccer players are semi-professional and Holland has one professional tennis player, Tom Okker. All other sports are strictly amateur.

There are eighteen clubs in the major soccer league, the top teams being Feyenoord (Rotterdam), Ajax (Amsterdam), ADO (The Hague), PSV (Philips Sport Vereniging of Eindhoven) and FC Twente (Enschede). In recent years the national championships has been won either by Feyenoord or Ajax, who have a tremendous following, not only in their home towns but all over Europe. The recent 2-0 victory of Ajax over Internazionale Milan (May 1972) has won Holland the European Cup for the third year in succession. Feyenoord beat Celtic (UK) in 1970, and Ajax defeated Panathinaikos (Greece) in 1971.

In cycling the main interest lies in international events. Great was the excitement when in 1968 a Dutch competitor, Jan Janssen, won the coveted *Tour de France*. Hopes are now centred on an up-and-coming cyclist, Joop Zoetemelk. Weekend cycling events are organised by the many amateur clubs all over the country and are especially popular in Limburg and Brabant. As a form of family recreation the bicycle is fast losing out to the car, but it is by no means rare on a Sunday afternoon to meet a family convoy pedalling sedately through the woods or dunes, the babies and younger children (and the dog) strapped into baskets in front of and behind their parents.

Skating may be termed a national sport, not only because nearly all Dutch children learn to skate, but also because Holland has frequently done well in European and world championships. Kees Verkerk and Sjoukje Dijkstra are former world champions, and Ard Schenk, the 1971 world champion, made sporting history by winning three gold medals in the 1972 Olympics.

There are excellent indoor and outdoor artificial rinks, but it is when the canals and lakes freeze that skating in Holland really comes into its own. Schoolchildren get special afternoon 'ice holidays' and are joined by every enthusiast who can wangle leave or mortgage some of his annual holiday in advance. The major event then is the *Elfstedentocht*, or Eleven Towns' Race, in Friesland, in which thousands of skaters from all over the country compete. Prizes are awarded to those who make the fastest time, and medals to everyone who completes the 125-mile long feat of endurance. A very small number do! Excitement mounts as the race gets under way, for this is the Dutch equivalent of the Grand National, the Monte Carlo Rally or the *Tour de France*.

Swimming is another sport in which the Dutch have taken international honours. Ada Kok held the 1969 world championship for women's butterfly stroke in the 100 and 200 metres. Swimming lessons are compulsory for all primary schoolchildren between the ages of ten and twelve. Facilities are good and have improved in the last ten years: in September 1970 there were 534 outdoor and 122 indoor pools. Many of the outdoor pools are heated.

Facilities for all water sports abound, and special recreation areas are being reserved for this purpose in the newly reclaimed parts of the country. Sailing, once the sport of the privileged few, is now within the reach of many through clubs and sailing schools.

The most widely played team games are volley ball, hockey, and a game resembling basketball which the Dutch call *korfbal*. The nearest equivalent to American baseball is *honkbal*. Rugby football and cricket are played only on a small scale; ice hockey is becoming more popular.

There are an enormous number of walking clubs. As many as 20,000 people, young and old, take part annually in the Nijmegen *Vierdaagse*, or four-day walk. In the north, an unusual and sometimes dangerous sport—*wadlopen*—consists of walking across the mud flats from the mainland to the Wadden Islands at certain tides.

Other active sports include amateur athletics, ice sailing, tennis and two sports peculiar to Friesland: *kaatsen*, a game rather like fives, and *polstokspringen*, or pole vaulting, originally the farmers' only means of crossing ditches and waterlogged land, now a local competitive sport. The British may be surprised to learn (and reluctant to admit) that the Dutch invented the game of golf, once called *kolf*. The turf, however, makes little appeal in Holland, although there are several racecourses. The Dutch Grand Prix motor race is held annually at Zandvoort, and TT racing is centred at Assen. Fishing is the most universally popular of the non-competitive sports.

Among indoor sports, gymnastics has always been prominent, but in the last few years, following the success of Anton Geesink, who became the first European to beat the Japanese, there has been a vogue for judo. There are now judo clubs in almost every town. American ten-pin bowling and skittles are also gaining popularity.

Facilities for all sports improve year by year, especially in so far as indoor accommodation is concerned, and the government keeps a watchful eye on the proper training of instructors.

AMUSEMENTS

The Dutch family is a close-knit unit which demands little diversion outside the home. For one thing, in the long, raw winter evenings there is little incentive to venture out of doors, and for another they do not care to spend large sums of money on entertainment. Thus they tend to make their own amusements in the winter months—they are great readers and television watchers—and when the sun shines they seem to enjoy it most in an unsophisticated way by strolling along the sea boulevards and in the parks, or by spending an hour or two on a café terrace.

Regular concert and theatre going is these days beyond the pockets of all but the professional and upper classes, but the cinema has retained its popularity in spite of television. The adolescents have their own diversions, principally their 'beat' groups and *discothèques*, the playboys the gay night life of the big cities and seaside resorts, although this is chiefly a tourist attraction. In between the two, the bulk of the people spread their patronage of public entertainment, other than the cinema, rather thinly throughout the year, and a night out at a show or dinner in a good restaurant is usually in celebration of some special occasion. Only the southern provinces go wild at the carnival season.

The great family festival is the feast of *Sint Nicolaas*, celebrated on the evening of 5 December. For weeks beforehand the children are in a fever of excitement, and the shops are full of marzipan novelties which are given as 'joke' presents alongside the real gifts. Most children are on their best behaviour at this time, lest Black Peter, the saint's negro assistant, should put them in his huge sack; for about two weeks before the festival they put shoes containing sugar and carrots for St Nicolas's horse in the fireplace at night and are sometimes rewarded by small gifts of chocolate and spiced biscuits the next morning. On the evening itself, parcels are opened in the family circle. Presents are given anonymously, or rather in the name of St Nicolas, and each gift is accompanied by a poem written by the donor, usually with some relevance to the good and bad characteristics of the recipient and to what he or she has done during the year. The poems are read out loud, and traditionally no one may become angry even if the content is not flattering; often it is very humorous. The news bulletins and weather forecast on TV and radio that evening are given partly in rhyme.

Except on the stock exchange, the Dutch are not great gamblers. Gaming houses were operated some years ago, but the Protestants in parliament have always voted against them and they were closed after a short time. The Dutch man in the street contents himself with a modest flutter on the football pools, the State lottery or the horse racing tote, which is the only form of betting allowed at race meetings; the more inveterate gambler goes to Belgium or Germany. The *Sport Toto*, or football pool, is operated by the Royal Netherlands Football Union under the authorisation of the State. Profits on the pools, together with those on the horse totes, are distributed annually among the national sports associations and used for the building of new

stadiums and other facilities. Most people buy a State lottery
ticket which costs 25 guilders, between several friends or members
of the family, or they can buy a fifth share. There are six draws
in the year. The top prize has been raised to 500,000 guilders
(just under £60,000 $156,000) in an attempt to attract those
who have hitherto participated only in the German lottery, which
offers higher prizes.

PUBLIC ENTERTAINMENT

Radio and television

Ninety-eight per cent of all Dutch homes have at least one
radio set, and 73 per cent have television. Very roughly this
amounts to twenty-one TV sets per hundred people. The exact
number of radio sets is impossible to ascertain, since a television
licence, which costs £9 ($23.40) for colour or black and white,
includes an unlimited number of radios in the one household. A
radio licence alone costs £3 ($7.80) a year. Deaf people and
those with very low incomes are exempt.

The broadcasting service is financed partly by the revenue
from licences and partly by that of the programme journals
published by the various broadcasting companies. The post office
runs a wire broadcasting system with four lines, one of which is
devoted entirely to popular music and another to classical music
from abroad, but this service is likely to end in 1973.

Colour television (the PAL system) started officially on 2
October 1967; transmission has now been increased to about
forty-five hours weekly. The number of colour TV sets in the
country is estimated at five hundred thousand.

When the Broadcasting Act became effective in May 1969, the
Netherlands Radio Union (NRU) and the Netherlands Television
Foundation (NTS) merged to form the Netherlands Broadcasting
Foundation (NOS). This central body is now responsible for
filling up to 40 per cent of TV transmitting time and up to 25
per cent of radio time, and for allocating the remainder among
the licensed broadcasting organisations. At far back as 1919,

when Dutch radio first went on the air, there have been five autonomous broadcasting organisations : AVRO (general), KRO (Catholic), NCRV (Protestant), VARA (Socialist), which is the largest, and VPRO (which used to be Liberal-Protestant). Two more recently licensed organisations are the non-denominational Television Radio Broadcasting Foundation (TROS) and the new Evangelical Broadcasting Organisation (EO).

Time on the air is allocated to the different companies according to their size; the churches, political parties, educational broadcasting services and certain opinion-forming societies share a maximum of 10 per cent. Advertising is controlled by the Foundation for Broadcast Advertising (STER), which is allowed up to 3 hours 15 minutes per week on television, divided between Nederland 1 and Nederland 2, and 3 hours 36 minutes on radio, divided between the three networks, Hilversum 1, 2 and 3.

The State exercises no control over programme content, except to ensure that they do not offend public law and order or morals. The breakdown of radio broadcasts is roughly 40 per cent spoken word, 35 per cent light music, 25 per cent serious music. One of the most successful Dutch programmes of recent years, *De Fabeltjeskrant* ('The Daily Fable'), with its bewitching owl storyteller and animal characters, ran daily for nearly two years up to the end of May 1970; public demand then brought it back for a further series. Intended originally for children, the programme became a special favourite of the men, with pride of place just before the main evening news bulletin. It may soon appear on British and other screens. Plays and serials are mostly imported from the United Kingdom, the United States, Germany, and a few from Belgium. In the south and east of Holland there is excellent reception of Belgian and German television.

The light music programmes of 'Radio Veronica,' and 'Radio Nordsee,' the pirate stations which operate from outside Dutch territorial waters in the North Sea, are very popular.

Radio Nederland, the World Broadcasting Service, broadcasts on the short wave in Dutch, Afrikaans, Indonesian, English, Arabic and Spanish.

The cinema

Dutch cinemas claim 37 per cent of the total revenue from all box office takings in the country, including those for sporting events. Attendances have gone down however—from 55 million to 24 million a year in the last twelve years—and in a move to ease the situation the government abolished entertainment tax in January 1969.

At least half the feature films shown come from the United States, the rest from Germany, the United Kingdom, France and Italy. All are given in their original sound with Dutch sub-titles. Because of the language difficulty, feature films produced in Holland are rarely seen outside that country, yet a number of them have won prizes at international film festivals, such as Fons Rademaker's *Village on the River*, which was nominated for an Oscar in 1959, and Philo Bregstein's *The Compromise*, which won a prize at the 1968 Venice Film Festival. In the documentary film world the work of Bert Haanstra and Herman van der Horst especially has won international acclaim. Financial help from the State and the growth of the television market has encouraged some of the younger film-makers like Adriaan Ditvoorst and René Daalder to experiment with short feature films.

Production costs at the Cinetone studios near Amsterdam are lower than in many other countries, and the Dutch film-maker is able to draw on the Film Production Fund, which was set up in 1956 to foster the production of Dutch feature films and to which the government and the Netherlands Cinema League contribute annually. The government also puts aside a certain sum each year (in 1968 it was nearly £10,000, $24,000) with which to finance independent directors of short films; the grants are made on the recommendation of the Arts Council Film Committee.

Music

Whether their taste is for classical or light music, jazz or 'pop,' the Dutch take their music seriously. Fewer households possess pianos than before the war, but this is a reflection on modern cramped living rather than on the musicality of the people. It is still unusual to come across a family in which no one plays an instrument, even if this turns out to be the recorder or guitar so beloved by the younger generation. And everyone stops to listen to the old street organ as it churns out the old favourites one after the other.

The winter subscription concerts of the *Concertgebouw Orkest* of Amsterdam, the *Residentie Orkest* of The Hague and the Rotterdam *Philharmonisch Orkest* are fully booked weeks before the season opens. These orchestras, the *Nederlands Kamerorkest* and the provincial orchestras receive substantial subsidies from the government and from their local authorities. The universities and *conservatoires* have their own orchestras, every town of any size its amateur philharmonic orchestra, chamber music or choral society, every village its local band. Competition is fierce, standards are high. Church music plays an important role in Dutch cultural life, and during Easter week there are memorable performances of Bach's *St Matthew Passion* in many churches.

Jazz, forbidden by the Germans during the war, came into its own from 1945 onwards with the formation of the Dutch Swing College Band and has also received a State subsidy. The modern vogue for 'beat' and folk music finds expression in groups such as The Cats, The Shocking Blue, The Golden Earrings and The Shoes.

The greatest name in Dutch music is the seventeenth-century composer, Jan Pieterzoon Sweelinck. Few others are known outside Holland, although in this century the work of Alphonse Diepenbrock and Willem Pijper has been of significance and encouragement to the present generation of musicians. Much of the work of the modern composers—Kees van Baaren, Ton de Leeuw, Peter Schat and a pioneer in electronic music, Henk Badings—is published by the Stichting Donemus, a government-sponsored foundation established to promote Dutch music.

The outstanding cultural event of the year, the Holland Festival, is held in June-July. Inaugurated in 1947 and covering music, drama and dance, it was at one time rated as one of the

K

major European festivals. Unfortunately its spectacular earlier successes have not been maintained, but it continues courageously to stage some first-class experimental productions.

Opera and ballet

Holland has no long-established opera or ballet tradition, no national opera house. *De Nederlandse Opera*, founded in 1946, gives 60 per cent of its performances in the Amsterdam *Schouwburg* (theatre) and in Rotterdam, The Hague and Utrecht. About 80 per cent of the seats are usually sold, half being guaranteed by subscription. The deficit is covered jointly by the State and the municipality. The *Zuid-Nederlandse Opera* of Maastricht tours the southern provinces, and a government-subsidised group, the *Forum*, based at Enschede, performs in the north and east. Recently there has been a flourishing of contemporary Dutch opera. Two singers who have achieved international success are Gré Brouwestijn and Christina Deutekom.

Ballet has been officially sponsored in Holland only for the last fifteen years, and public interest has been aroused after a long, hard struggle. The Dutch National Ballet, the Netherlands Dance Theatre and the Scapino Ballet now receive financial help from the government and from the municipalities of Amsterdam and The Hague. The participation of Rudolf Nureyev in recent productions of the National Ballet, and the enthusiastic reception these companies have received at home and abroad, speaks for itself.

The National Ballet, formed in 1961, owes much to Sonia Gaskell, founder of the earlier 'Ballet Recital' group. Since her retirement in 1968, artistic direction of the company has been in the hands of two young choreographers, Rudi van Dantzig and Robert Kaesen. Its repertoire is both classical and modern and includes a number of Balanchine ballets. The company also dances with the Netherlands Opera.

The Netherlands Dance Theatre began in 1959 as a small group of dancers who had separated from Sonia Gaskell's ballet in order to devote themselves to contemporary and experimental work; it is now regarded as one of the more important dance companies of Europe.

For young people there is the Scapino Ballet, a unique company formed soon after the liberation in 1945 under the direction of Mrs Hans Snoek. Scapino, the lovable jester from the *Commedia dell 'Arte*, explains the stories to the audience and dances in the ballets. The dancers are all Dutch, and about 90 per cent of their repertoire is specially commissioned work by Dutch musicians and designers.

Theatre

Every year the government pays out substantial grants to some fifteen professional theatre companies. Without this aid, the theatre in Holland could not survive. The three major companies, *De Nederlandse Comedie, De Haagse Comedie* and *Het Nieuw Rotterdams Toneel*, receive financial aid to cover their operational deficits in the ratio of 40 per cent from the State and 60 per cent from the municipalities of Amsterdam, The Hague and Rotterdam respectively. The various regional companies get special grants or funds to encourage them to tour the country.

Basically, the Dutch are not theatregoers. The language difficulty, which means that even if a play enjoys reasonable success in its native country it has practically no chance of a tour abroad, affords little incentive to Dutch writers to work in the theatre. The majority of plays performed are translations of British, American, French or German successes. An exception is the work of Hugo Claus, a modern Belgian playwright writing in Flemish.

The most exciting development recently has been the opening of an experimental theatre (HOT) in The Hague in November 1969. Housed in a former church, it has been planned as a cultural centre and is open from mid-morning until after midnight.

THE VISUAL ARTS

The rich historical and art heritage of Holland is contained in almost 500 museums, a large number of which are art galleries. Seven million people visit these museums annually, three million more than the number who go to concerts, the theatre, opera and ballet. Statistics do not reveal how many of these are tourists, but every year art lovers by the thousand come from all over the world to see the Dutch treasures. The recent Rembrandt ter-centenary exhibition at the *Rijksmuseum* in Amsterdam attracted long queues of people nearly every day.

It is impossible here to do more than mention some of the great names in Dutch art. The van Eyck brothers are generally regarded as founders of the Flemish School which flourished in the fifteenth century. Hieronymus Bosch, Lucas van Leyden and Pieter Brueghel the Elder were outstanding in the sixteenth century, towards the end of which portrait painting, especially group portraiture, began to be fashionable. The following hun-dred years represent the 'Golden Age,' immortalised in the work of the great artists Rembrandt, Vermeer and Hals, the gentle landscapes of van Goyen and Ruysdael, the interior and court-yard settings of Pieter de Hoogh, and a host of others.

A rather anaemic period during the eighteenth century was followed by the emergence of J. B. Jongkind, one of the early Impressionists, towards the middle of the nineteenth century, and some years later by the romantic style of painting that became known as The Hague School, led by Jacob Maris and Hendrik Mesdag. Then came the individualist Vincent Van Gogh and, at the turn of the century, the Amsterdam Impressionists headed by G. H. Breitner and Josef Israels gave way to the symbolists Jan Toorop and J. Thorn Prikker.

The early 1920s saw the formation of *De Stijlgroep* of artists and architects who took their name from the *avant-garde* maga-zine of the immediate post-war period, which was to have the most far-reaching influence, not merely in Holland, but on the whole of modern European and American art. Prominent in this move-ment were Piet Mondriaan, considered to be Holland's greatest twentieth-century painter, Theo van Doesburg, Bart van der Leck, and the architects J. J. P. Oud, H. P. Berlage and W. M. Dudok, who sought to bring a new simplicity into the art form through the use of uncluttered lines and rectangular shapes, and by painting in the primary colours. By this time the Dutch painter, Kees van Dongen, had established himself in Paris.

The Expressionists of the inter-war period (Hendrik Chabot, Herman Kruyder, Jan Sluyters) were of national rather than international importance, and in 1948 there came the Experimental group of painters and poets founded by Appel, Corneille and Constant. Among the moderns, Jaap Wagemaker is known for his 'unorthodox' paintings and Maurits Escher is one of the world's best graphic artists.

Sculpture does not have a great tradition in Holland, but has come to the fore since the last war. Wessel Couzijn's massive 'Corporate Unity' stands in the forecourt of the new Unilever headquarters in Rotterdam; Mari Andriessen has produced some striking monuments to those who lost their lives in the war and in the 1953 flood disaster.

In architecture Holland was always well known for her distinctive gabled houses of the seventeenth and eighteenth centuries. Berlage, architect of the Amsterdam stock exchange, was the first to break with tradition. The functionalists followed, and simplicity of structure, together with the experimental use of building materials, especially glass, characterised the years immediately preceding World War II. Today there are some outstanding examples of the best modern architecture in Europe among the town halls, schools, congress centres, concert halls and country houses of Holland. Colour is much used, and also glass and ceramics, for which the Dutch are world famous. Because many towns in the west are built on a foundation of piles thrust into the ground, skyscrapers are not possible. One of the tallest buildings is the new eighteen-storey Ministry of Cultural Affairs, Recreation and Social Welfare at Rijswijk, near The Hague.

Industry and the government between them commission a fair proportion of works of art. In all new buildings put up by the State, $1\frac{1}{2}$ per cent of the cost of construction is spent on works of art, 1 per cent in the case of schools or other educational establishments. The government supports artists through prizes, commissions, exhibitions and grants to art institutions; it also operates a subsidy scheme for private buyers of works of art, under which the organisers of certain government-approved exhibitions are guaranteed a subsidy for a year, enabling them to offer a 25 per cent rebate to Dutch purchasers of works by living Dutch artists priced up to £350 ($840). The buyer has to sign an undertaking that he will not dispose of the work within five years of its purchase. The exhibition organiser pays the artist the full price and is reimbursed by the government.

LITERATURE

Dutch writing is relatively unknown outside Holland, except in Belgium, South Africa and Indonesia. Erasmus and Grotius in their time had to write in Latin in order to reach a wide public; some modern Dutch authors have turned to English. Not long ago Dutch literature was predominantly provincial, moralising and narrow-minded. Today it has swung to the other extreme, and some people consider it much too ruthless, too outspoken.

Three-quarters of all books published are first editions; in 1970, out of a total of 11,159 titles, 1,550 were original Dutch novels or collections of poetry. Bookshops abound in all the large towns and do brisk business. The public libraries, which are government-subsidised, lend nearly 46 million books a year. As in Britain, writers are pressing for public lending rights.

The greatest figure in Dutch letters is the seventeenth-century poet-playwright, Joost van den Vondel, but his works, unlike those of Shakespeare, to whom he has been compared, are rarely performed. The poetic tradition has continued down the centuries and found a new form in the work of some Resistance poets of the last war.

The first to break through the insipid writing of the mid-nineteenth century was Eduard Douwes Dekker, whose novel *Max Havelaar*, published in 1860 under the pen-name 'Multatuli,' created a sensation by the forceful clarity of its style. At the turn of the century, Louis Couperus, the pioneer of the psychological novel, was at first underrated, but was recognised some years later as a European novelist of distinction. A landmark in the development of a new literary movement took place in the 1930s, when some critics and younger writers revolted against the 'pretty' writing then in vogue. After the last war Anna Blaman and 'Simon' (now Gerard Kornelis) van het Reve led the way.

The most prolific Dutch writer alive today is the versatile Simon Vestdijk, who for more than thirty years has been pouring out a stream of novels, essays and short stories. Hella Haasse and Adriaan van der Veen, Willem Frederik Hermans and Harry Mulisch are representative of the post-war generation, while much controversy surrounds the young Jan Cremer, recently awarded the state prize for literature, whose uncouth idiom sets out to shock. The Dutch authors best known to English readers are Johan Fabricius and Jan de Hartog.

Government aid takes the form of annual literary awards, travel grants, a certain amount of commissioned work and the promotion of the translation of Dutch works into the major world languages.

The multilingual Dutch prefer to read books in their original text, and bookshops carry a stock of English, French and German titles. Best-sellers and the most popular foreign books generally appear in Dutch paperback editions.

THE PRESS

Ninety-seven per cent of all Dutch newspapers are sold by subscription and delivered to subscribers' homes. Some tobacconists, supermarkets and town railway kiosks also sell papers and magazines, and newsvendors representing individual papers visit cafés and restaurants. Because the majority of papers are evening editions, the Dutchman does not, unlike the Englishman or American, read his daily paper over breakfast or on the way to work; he mostly reads it at home in the evening, or at a café where, if he is so disposed, he may spend several hours over a beer or cup of coffee reading the various papers provided. At a weekly subscription of approximately 25p (65 US cents), the Dutch newspaper is one of the cheapest in western Europe. Ninety-four per cent of all households, including people living alone, take at least one daily paper.

The national dailies (which in Holland means those published in Amsterdam or Rotterdam) are the independent *De Telegraaf*, *Nieuws van de Dag* and *Algemeen Dagblad*, the socialist *Het Vrije Volk* and *Het Parool*, the Roman Catholic *De Tijd* and *De Volkskrant*, the Protestant *Trouw*, and the liberal *Nieuwe Rotterdamse Courant* with which the *Algemeen Handelsblad* recently merged. Some publish regional editions, and there are independent provincial papers such as the *Haagsche Courant* which have an even larger circulation than the nationals. Most local papers read in the south are Roman Catholic; elsewhere they are in the main non-sectarian.

Holland does not have the sensational press of America or the United Kingdom. *De Telegraaf*, which is a morning paper, is the only one to report in this style, and for this reason it is often attacked in political circles. It has the largest circulation, and many office workers glance at it before getting down to the day's business.

The Netherlands Newspaper Press Association (NDP) was founded in 1906. In 1935 it established the General Netherlands Press Agency (ANP), which supplies national and foreign papers with news items and runs the radio news service. Most journalists belong to the Netherlands Union of Journalists (NVJ), a merger of the former Catholic, Protestant and non-sectarian journalistic associations.

There is concern in government and press circles over the increasing number of newspaper mergers, and the Press Council has made recommendations to the Ministry for Cultural Affairs that may lead to a new Press Act. Meanwhile the government spends about 15 million guilders a year to help various newspapers which would otherwise no longer be economically viable on account of rising costs and the loss of advertising to television.

A unique press centre, the *Nieuwspoort*, at the Binnenhof in

The Hague, was opened in 1962. Its facilities are available to pressmen of all nationalities, who make full use of its proximity to the two chambers of the States-General and the cabinet, often the sources of 'hot news.'

Weekly opinion papers include the liberal *Elseviers Weekblad* and the *Haagse Post*, the socialist *Vrij Nederland* and another left-wing paper, *De Groene Amsterdammer*. Illustrated weeklies are *De Spiegel*, *Wereld-Kroniek*, *Panorama* and *Revu*. Businessmen mostly read *Het Financiale Dagblad*.

According to a recent survey, the typical Dutch man or woman spends three-quarters of an hour each day reading the paper. Many also read monthly and weekly journals, including those of other countries. Seventy per cent of the total female population over the age of fifteen reads one or more of the popular women's weeklies, *Eva*, *Libelle*, *Princes* or *Margriet*. The better-class monthly glossy magazines are *Avenue*, *Elegance* and *De Vrouw en haar Huis*.

STATE AID

When the Ministry of Cultural Affairs, Recreation and Social Welfare was established in 1965, it assumed overall responsibility for the promotion of the cultural and social well-being of the Dutch people, tasks which had formerly been handled by the Ministry of Education, Arts and Sciences and the Ministry of Social Welfare.

The amount of money spent by the Ministry increases year by year, and it now represents about 5.1 per cent of total government expenditure.

8

Hints For Visitors

WHEN

CHOOSE April and the first half of May for the bulbfields, but do not count on the tulips being out if Easter is early, it depends on the year; June for the Holland Festival and reasonably uncluttered beaches; July, August and the beginning of September for family seaside holidays (avoid Scheveningen and the big resorts in July); all the year round for sightseeing, shopping, museums and concerts. Gourmets may enjoy plovers' eggs in early April, asparagus in May, the new herring in June.

Whatever the season, take a warm coat and suitable rainwear. Heavy showers often occur in the summer months.

Advance booking is essential in spring and summer and advisable at other times. Lists of hotel and other accommodation are published by the ANVV (Netherlands National Tourist Office), Mauritskade 17, The Hague. Every town has a VVV (local tourist information office), recognisable by its triangular blue sign with white lettering. In the main holiday centres the VVV will assist visitors in finding accommodation. The Amsterdam VVV runs a special service, 'Get in touch with the Dutch,' for those who want to make personal contact with the people.

SOCIAL CUSTOM

Holland is a hospitable country, and the foreign visitor may well be invited to a Dutch home. There are three golden rules : be punctual, go armed with a small gift for your hostess (flowers, a pot plant or chocolates are usual), shake hands with everyone present on arrival and on departure. When introductions are made, the Dutch always shake hands and say their surname. The Englishman's polite 'How do you do?' will almost certainly be taken literally and answered in detail. He should, however, try not to look surprised when greeted informally in the street with a bright 'Good-bye!' The Hollander has only the one word, *dag*, meaning both 'Hallo' and 'Good-bye.'

When invited to spend Sunday with friends, it is wise to follow the Dutch custom of eating a hearty breakfast beforehand—there is no traditional Sunday lunch here as in Britain, and you may not be offered anything substantial to eat until early evening.

One of the worst sins you can commit is to ignore a friend's birthday. If you need to check up on a date, remember that every household has hanging in the downstairs lavatory (presumably as a useful daily reminder) a special calendar listing not only the birthdays of friends and relations, but also their own! Take or send flowers or a small present if a close friend, otherwise telephone or write a card. In Holland flowers are given as much to men as to women.

Less formal than the Germans, the Dutch still tend to be stiffer than the English and Americans in their everyday manners. The use of Christian names among colleagues and neighbours is slowly becoming more widespread under the influence of the modern generation, whose parents, however, cling to the old and extremely complicated conventions relating to written modes of address. The foreigner, unless he is absolutely sure of the correct form, would be well advised to shelter behind the English 'Mr . . .', which is quite acceptable.

The Dutch way of telling the time causes some confusion to English-speaking people. They say *half twee* (literally 'half two') meaning half past one, ie half before two o'clock. Similarly, *half tien* is nine-thirty, *half ses* is half past five.

MOTORING

There are any number of petrol and service stations, many of which sell motor accessories, maps, sweets and soft toys. All the normal grades of petrol are available, and the pump attendant automatically cleans your windscreen. The red Michelin 'Benelux' guide is very reliable; the best maps are produced by KNAC (Royal Dutch Automobile Club) and ANWB, and these may be purchased by non-members. Cheaper and less detailed, but adequate, are folder maps printed by the big oil companies, on sale at garages and filling stations.

Except on motorways and priority roads (marked with an orange diamond sign), you must give way to traffic coming from the right: remember especially that the British rule of priority for vehicles already on a roundabout does not apply. When turning off right, watch for cyclists coming down the cycle path, as they have precedence.

TIPPING

Hotels, restaurants and hairdressers include a 12½-15 per cent service charge, and their staff usually say '*inclusief*' when presenting the bill. In luxury restaurants, or where the service has been exceptionally good, it is usual to leave the odd small change. Taxi drivers add 15-20 per cent on to the meter charge. For the rest, porters expect a minimum of 50 Dutch cents per piece of luggage, wardrobe attendants 25 cents to one guilder (depending on the class of establishment), lavatory attendants 25 cents. Some people tip cinema or theatre ushers, but this is unnecessary.

Bibliography

The Common Market and the Common Man, (1971, European Communities, Brussels)

The Kingdom of the Netherlands: Facts and Figures, (1971, Government Printing Office, The Hague)

Jaarboek Grote Winkler Prins, (1969, 1970)

Manpower and Social Policy in the Netherlands, (1967, OECD, Paris)

Netherlands (OECD Economic Survey), (1968, Paris)

Statistisch Zakboek 1970, 1971, (Centraal Bureau voor de Statistiek, The Hague)

Van twee tot twee miljoen auto's in Nederland, (1969, Centraal Bureau voor de Statistiek, The Hague)

BAENA, DUKE DE *The Dutch Puzzle*, (1968, 5th edition, The Hague)

HUGGETT, F. E. *The Modern Netherlands*, (1971, London)

MATERS, J. C. *Wat verdienen wij in Nederland?*, (1967 Deventer)

PATHUIS, H. AND VAN DER SPEEK J. *The Netherlands Work and Prosperity*, (1967, 2nd edition, Zeist)

SCHÖFFER, I. *A Short History of the Netherlands*, (1956, Amsterdam)

VAN WEL, FREEK. *Holland*, (1969, Hanover)

Index